TAKING IN THE VIEW

Life from a Scooter

Copyright © Mark Bennett 2023

Round the Bend Publications
www.lifefromascooter.com

ISBN 978-1-3999-6637-5

For my children; Evie, Tess, Issy and Arthur

So that they can see what their old dad got up to when he was a kid

And continues to do now.

THE ROAD TO RACK & RUIN

Riding up a steep mountain pass in the Alps, my scooter's headlight reflects off the wet shiny road.

The light rain has morphed into a thunderous and torrential downpour, water streams down the road towards me, lightning flashes and I am wet to the skin, still miles from anywhere.

A satnav instruction comes through my headset, "you have reached your destination, turn around and follow the road."

What? No!

I curse, loudly and repeatedly.

Realising my mistake, I perform a U-turn, gently wind the throttle open and forlornly retrace my route back down the mountainside…

PART 1
FROM THE BEGINNING...

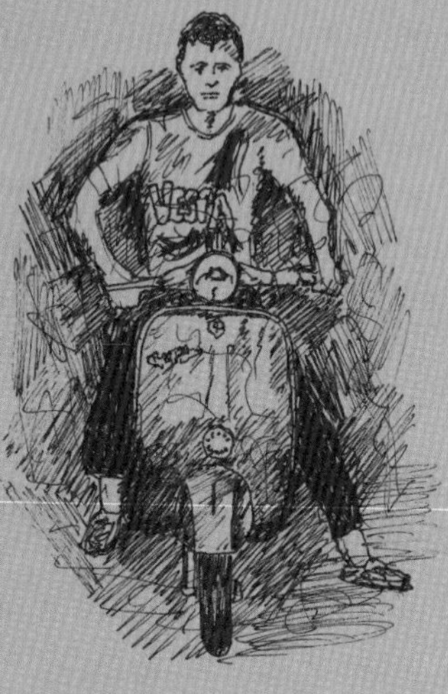

TO BE SOMEONE

It is 1982 and a 13-year-old lad influenced by school mates has found something in the music of The Specials, Madness and The Jam. What it is he does not know yet, or where it will lead him, but it gives him some sort of identity that growing up in a small East Anglian village, the eldest child of working class Liverpudlian parents, had not been able to provide up till then. He regularly finds himself feeling separate from other kids in the village and at school and is constantly trying to find his place in his own small world. It will be a while before he finds that place.

This isolated lad is me and I was far from unique at the time. Many young people in the early 1980s found excitement, influence, and direction in the various youth cultures of post-punk England, in the clothing that set them apart from others and the rebellious music that made their pulses race but confused their parents. The music also provided the icons and heroes whose posters would plaster my bedroom walls, whether my little brother wanted them to or not, sharing that space with Airfix model planes that hung from the ceiling with the aid of drawing pins and thread. This was the time though that the model making, football up at the rec with jumpers for goalposts and games of war on the building site behind the family council house, would soon be replaced by searching out new bands in the pages of the NME and Smash Hits, rushing home to catch the latest appearance of one of these new bands miming on Top of the Pops or having my musical world expanded by John Peel late at night on Radio 1, which would then be followed by a bicycle ride into Cambridge on a Saturday to visit Andy's Records, Jay's or Our Price, to buy the new finds or to The Beat Goes On to rifle through rows and rows of old vinyl records in the basement, looking for something that I just had to have in my ever expanding record collection.

And of course, any self-respecting and rebellious teenager could not be seen in any old clobber. Whatever the latest clothing to be seen in was, some funds would be needed. Those funds would come from pocket money, a couple of paper rounds and a Saturday job, or repeatedly hassling poor old Mum and Dad because I could not live without the latest black Harrington jacket or tasselled loafers until they gave in and took me to Barneys on Mill Road to get kitted out using the child benefit money. I remember the racks of Sta-prest trousers there, in a multitude of colours along with donkey jackets, button down shirts, cardigans (both Y and waffle) and whatever else made up the necessary threads for a boy (or girl) about town. Mates were occasionally roped in when I was working on a Saturday to traipse across town and pick up some recently ordered shoes for me (think red, white and blue Jam stage shoes) or the polka dot button-down shirt I had ordered from Carnaby Street.

Two 7" singles, Ghost Town by The Specials (still completely relevant today) and the Bad Manners ska-ish version of the Can Can, made my first foray into buying records considered cool by my peers, rather than the Christmas present from a grandparent of The Shadow's String of Hits LP from 1979. If you are old enough you might remember the one, it had a stylised Fender Stratocaster made to look like it had the needle tracks from a record adorning the guitar body and was not considered worthy by any young teenager that was trying to be rebelliously cool!

The record that was to be the catalyst for a hobby (some would say lifestyle) that would play a major part in my life from the age of 16, giving me an enviable working knowledge of the UK road network worthy of any Little Chef or Happy Eater route map, was bought as one of a pair. To this day I still struggle to buy just one record on its own and so along with Live at the Marquee by the fantastic English blues band Nine Below Zero, I purchased another album which still sends me instantly back to the time I first lifted the needle of a cheap record player onto the black disc with its red, white and blue roundel label.

The band were The Jam, the sound was crisp and smart and came from a long way away from my little world. The opening title track "All Mod Cons", which lasted for all of one minute and 20 seconds, still makes me tingle to this day with its opening slashes of guitar chords and reverb that packed such a powerful punch. That long playing record blew my naïve teenage mind and took me via acoustic love songs, feedback drenched sagas and tales of class difference all the way through to the violent but sublime masterpiece of "Down in the Tube Station at Midnight". It is the LP record that is still my undisputed favourite and unwittingly influenced where I was to go in my life.

But it was not the just the music that had such a dramatic effect on me. Take the album in your hands, look at the cover, the sparse setting and three of the coolest people on the planet at that time. Then pull out the inner sleeve, holding the black vinyl disc and marvel at the collage of 1960's ephemera, records, badges and nick-nacks gathered together to display some of the band's influences and life and then turn the sleeve over. Read the stunning lyrics, written almost entirely by the 21-year-old, some would say genius some would say arrogant, Paul Weller and then look behind them to see a sparse line drawing.

Looking like it had been taken from a technical handbook written by a suit and tie wearing engineer of days gone by, it was of an Italian Vespa motor scooter. This almost subliminal picture was the spark that ignited the fuel and began the journey of scooters and me. It is still going strong over 40 years later, taking me all over Europe and the UK, introducing me along the way to a vast and eclectic range of people that I can call friends and thankfully, this "hobby" shows no signs of ending just yet, in fact it just keeps getting better and better. Long may it last.

My All Mod Cons LP and the inner sleeve with the Vespa diagram

LAMBRETTAVESPASCOOTER
MOD MOD MOD

At this point scooters were not an option due to my age, but the seed had been sown and that workshop manual image printed in blue ink was the literal shape of things to come. In the meantime, my push bike would remain as my main form of transport. I would concentrate on the music and the clothes whilst trying to find that place of belonging in the world that I looked for. The Jam would stylistically influence my wardrobe massively as well as my musical taste and outlook on life. The mod style of the late seventies would have the biggest bearing on my choice of clothing with a secondary influence coming from the sixties and the likes of the Small Faces and The Who.

I became something of a musical magpie. There is so much sparkly music out there that will make you laugh, cry, get angry, get even, mourn a lost love, or charm a new one, that sticking to one style and missing out on so much just makes no sense at all. A friend occasionally sends me a homemade (CD) mixtape or a spare copy of something he thinks I'll appreciate. When I finally got round to playing the Goldie Looking Chain CD that he had sent me, I couldn't help but belly laugh to the Welsh rapping humourists and their ingenious take on American urban culture, with songs like "Guns Don't Kill People, Rappers Do" and "Roller Disco", proving it's a big wide musical world out there.

Other bands would influence me too. Madness and The Specials would lead me on to ska from Jamaica, Nine Below Zero would introduce me to the Chicago blues of Otis Rush with their cover of "I Can't Quit You Baby" and the rock blues of Rory Gallagher's "Sugar Mama", whilst The Jam would give me The Small Faces; The Who, Tamla Motown, Wison Pickett, Otis Redding, Dr Feelgood, Gang of Four and so much more. But the Jam weren't just about music and style, they were attitude and intellect, they would constantly evolve, keeping their fan base on full alert, regularly changing direction. You could go that way too if you wanted, no one forced you, but it was a great ride if you did. That was The Jam.

And then there was a book. Not just any book but a book that returned me to that image first recognised on the inner sleeve of the All Mod Cons LP.

This book was not about the humble Italian motor scooter but about style, what to wear and what music to listen to. It became something of a bible for people wanting to visit those heady days of the 1960s but weren't able to, being born too late. The (mainly) Lambretta and Vespa scooters that featured heavily within the pages of this book were an accessory to the young people riding them but the scooters were also transport, independence and a way of getting to an English seaside resort with hordes of like-minded teenagers experiencing the growing distance between the austerity of post-war Britain and the need to make their own place in the modern world. The book was Mods! by Richard Barnes and like many others, I would spend hours flicking through its pages taking in the cut of the cloth, the styles of the haircuts and the camaraderie of the youngsters lucky enough to be there at that time. But over time, the music and scooters were where it was at for me. Clothing styles could change, and short hair could be grown but buying records, the newest release from the latest popular beat combo maybe or delving deeper into more diverse and exotic styles, and scooters, which would get me mobile (when it wasn't breaking down), would give me the chance to explore the big wide world that surrounded me, both literally and figuratively. A book on its own was not enough though. Moving pictures would make all the still photographs from the book come to life and show how these people moved, spoke, danced, and rode, so that I could do the same too.

In the small village that I grew up in, an altruistic parent spotted that local kids needed somewhere to gather in an evening and socialise in a different way to the usual hanging around on a street corner and so started up a youth club for us. It was somewhere that at the same time would give the surrounding residents of that street corner some respite from our shenanigans. We weren't bad kids but looking back we were probably louder than we realised and the regular unauthorised retrieval of a football from a garden or falling into a freshly pruned hedge while play fighting was probably a tad irritating for them while the loitering under a street light in front of their bedroom would either disturb their sleep patterns or disrupt their night-time amorous pursuits and so probably justified the occasional "oi you lot, bloody well clear off!"

A souvenir from Margate in the late 1980s

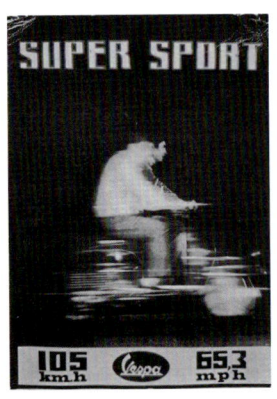

Book pictures used for bedroom wall decor

It was at this youth club that we were occasionally able to suggest a film that was reasonable to watch in the presence of responsible adults (if you pretended to gaze at your shoes through one or two particular scenes) but that maybe our own parents wouldn't even think of entertaining just in case it stopped their enjoyment of the Nine O'clock News or Coronation Street. There was only one option for a potential scooter riding teenage mod to suggest for what we could watch next. It was a film that I got to know of from the music of The Who and that was responsible for a huge influx of teenage wannabes into the mod scene and then the scooter scene at the time of its release. What else could "that" film have been but Quadrophenia?

Described online as "a 1979 British drama film loosely based on The Who's 1973 rock opera of the same name", Quadrophenia was so much more than that to so many young people. The music is stunning, Pete Townshend demonstrated his lyrical greatness within its songs and The Who, as an entity, totally blew the proverbial roof off the place right from the subtle opening of "I Am the Sea", which merged into the tightness of "The Real Me" and carried on all the way through to the sublime "Love, Reign O'er Me".

I couldn't play a musical instrument, however much I may or may not have practiced in front of a mirror (go on admit it, we've all done it!), so a career as a guitar wielding rock god was out of the question. But the characters being played in this crazy but "real" film set only 20 years before I was watching it, how they lived their lives and more importantly how and where they rode their scooters was totally achievable, even if it would often strip my bank account of any available funds in the coming years. The number of young men at the time that saw themselves as the Ace Face or Jimmy or the young women that felt they could have been Steph or Monkey must have been immense. And to top that, if you hung around in the scene long enough you would soon discover that real bona fide mods and scooterboys were paid to be extras in the film. It gave the feeling that every kid in the country that wanted to, could ride down to the coast for a bank holiday weekend of dancing and debauchery… "You goin' to Brighton this weekend?"

For me, the music was more rock than mod, but the influence that this film exerted over the teenage population in the five years or so following its release, cannot be underestimated. I know, I walked out of the youth club that night with one thing and one thing only in my mind. I wanted a scooter, whether it was a Lambretta or a Vespa didn't matter, but I wanted a scooter!

GET YOUR MOTOR RUNNING

I'm 16 years old and at the stage where school is not where I want to be. Overnight, I made the drastic decision that the career holding my interest up until that point, was not going to happen. Exams followed by college, followed by university, then more exams followed by years of training and countless more exams completely blew my brain. No one in my working class family had ever been to university before, that was for posh rich kids, so all I could think of doing at the time was to mess around at school, irritate the teachers and treat my exams with the contempt that I thought they deserved. How the young think they know everything!

My mind was full of the thought of expanding my world. I'd been to my first gig, Billy Bragg at the City Limits, a small pub venue in Cambridge, had dropped in to visit Carnaby Street on a school trip (that wasn't included on the itinerary!) and had started to notice older lads around town on scooters. Not just any old scooters though, these lads had sprayed them in metallic paints, adorned front mudguards with Jaguar bonnet mascots or painted their crash helmets with designs like the stars and stripes to catch the eye. One of them would be featured in the local newspaper after a police officer reported him, feeling his Jaguar mascot was a risk to pedestrians. Andy Hawes, who I got to know later, was cleared of the offence in court and carried on riding his decorated scooter. I would follow suit with my own roaring cat very soon after. This is where I wanted to be.

A few friends were into some of the music or clothes that I liked but no one seemed to know much about scooters. And while we would all jump up and down to "Too Much Too Young" or "Town Called Malice" in our Sta-prest and Fred Perry polo shirts at school discos, there was the US Army parkas and Levi jeans of the older scooters lads and other more exotic types of music that caught my attention too, think "Ace of Spades" by Motorhëad or "Janie Jones" by The Clash, which going by the clothes I wore I should not be listening too. What a shock I was soon going to get.

Some kids at school were able to get themselves mobile with the likes of a FS1E or SS50 moped, while one made do with a Puch Maxi and another, whose parents must have had a few quid more than others, had the luxury of a brand new Yamaha DT50MX with white bodywork, red frame, and a red seat. This was the machine that was to give me my first taste of two wheels and an engine as opposed to the pedal power that had transported me around so far. A small gang of us from the village had enthusiastically run the length of the High Street to meet Darren, the owner of the DT50, at the start of the rec road, a concrete track of about half a mile leading into the Fens and towards the local sewage works. Oh, the dizzying heights of teenage life! He sat proudly astride his bike as we took it in turns to twist the throttle open, the engine noise rising quickly then falling as the throttle was closed and the engine settled back to a steady idle. We must have been badgering him for five or ten minutes to let us all have a go before he relented and so, after a few others, I found myself sat astride this pinging two-stroke mean machine. I gave the kickstart a prod, followed the instructions to pull in the clutch lever, selected first gear with my left foot and then promptly dumped the clutch sending the front wheel skyward! The machine lurched forward, the wheel landed back on the concrete with a bounce and the engine came to a stalling halt after all of 20ft. A complete and utter disaster but I was well and truly hooked and wanted a scooter now more than ever.

I finished school at 16 years old in the summer of 1984 and my Saturday job, working in a bicycle shop, became my first full time employment paying me the grand total of about £45 a week. I then discovered the local Vespa dealer, Graham Jenkins Motorcycles, and would drop in to pick up brochures and gaze longingly at the scooters and accessories hooked up on the wall display. I must have given Dad a right old ear bashing before he eventually gave in and agreed to sign the hire purchase agreement allowing me to own my first scooter, but thankfully he did, and I duly ordered my first and very own scooter. Sensibly my parents insisted I take a new rider course with the local council run motorcycle trainer before I took to the road and then, on August the 1st 1984, they drove me to the shop to collect the shiny black Italian Vespa PK50S that would start me on my rollercoaster journey of owning and riding scooters. Papers were signed and keys handed over. My scooter (registration number B496 XFL) was wheeled to the front of the shop by one of the mechanics as I enthusiastically donned my open face helmet, and black scooter jacket. No problems with out of control wheelies this time. After having the basic controls of choke and petrol tap pointed out to me, I kickstarted the engine into life and sat on my first scooter. I dread to think what Mum and Dad were thinking at that moment, but with a wave and "see you at home," I set off across the junction and joined in with the other traffic. I can't remember exactly what I was told but remembered something about a running in period, returning in 500 miles time for the first service, so I gently made my way home successfully controlling the power of the mighty PK. I had finally arrived on the scooter riding map.

WRECKIN' CREW

Sixteen years old, working, mobile and independent (ish). How life changes in a very short time. Other kids would now look at my scooter, twist the throttle and endlessly ask "can I have a go?" I would ride around the village meeting mates who were still using pedal power, then venture into neighbouring villages without having to break into a sweat. It was an amazing care free time, protective clothing was limited to a Levi jacket, a cheap MA1 style flight jacket or a parka from the army surplus store (black without a hood for me), an open face crash helmet, Sta-prest, some smart shoes or maybe some boxing boots, but they were for the look and certainly not for safety. Gloves weren't thought of, unless it was cold, they just weren't cool. It mattered more how you looked when you were riding than how much it would hurt if you fell off, not that you really considered falling off as everyone knows you're protected by the invincibility of youth at that time in your life. In all honesty, the power that the Vespa PK50 wielded meant that I was probably at more risk of injury from falling off the kerb!

With other village mates who had recently turned 16 and got themselves moped mobile, I would buzz around in a group of smoke emitting machines thinking girls would now see us and swoon at our feet. How wrong we were. We were still awkward, gangly teenage boys who would lose the power of speech if just one good looking girl were to even look in our direction, so we continued racking up the miles in hope of a magical injection of charisma and confidence. Whilst the other lads on their mini motorcycles would spend their wages on a front gear sprocket to add a few more miles an hour to their top speed, or change the exhaust to one made by the legendary Micron, making it sound even more like a can containing an angry wasp, I would fritter away my measly wages on bolt on accessories to adorn the mighty PK and hope that I could also afford a visit into town to buy a few records on the way home, before I handed over a few quid to Mum for my rent. Even being on just £50 a week at that time and with my lack of money management skills, my wage seemed to go much further, especially when petrol cost pennies compared to the £2 a litre it reached in 2022, and the PK's engine was able to squeeze many miles out of a full tank.

As I've hinted, the Vespa PK50S is not renowned for its power and speed, riding a scooter then was about the look, so I can only hold that film first seen in the local youth club responsible for taking control over me and instilling the desire to bolt on every bit of chrome tatt I possibly could, further reducing the power to weight ratio of B496 XFL. Over a short period of time I would add, and here I need to take a deep breath; a smoked flyscreen, handlebar tassels, handlebar mirrors, yellow headlight paint, front crash bars, more mirrors, a Jaguar mudguard mascot, whitewall tyres, wheel discs, floor mats, Florida crash bars, an ironing board back rest, a whip aerial and a chequered mudflap. Along with all that I did try to unleash some power with an exhaust that probably slowed the engine if anything, but sounded great and the two small side panels were removed and chromed at the local electroplaters. After the PK, none of my scooters stayed plain or unmodified for long. There was always a need and desire to personalise them and that has always been a big part of the scooter scene too.

Riding through town at night, neon streetlights and car headlights sparkled on the chrome accessories fitted to my scooter and I would catch my reflection in the shop windows as I rode past. In my head, I was as cool as Jimmy riding his Lambretta in those opening scenes of Quadrophenia. Now that I had my own transport and didn't have to rely on a bus or my push bike, I could travel further afield, not just for the hell of it but also for work. I landed a job a few miles out of town in a wholesaler's warehouse that supplied tobacco and confectionery to local shops and newsagents. As a 16-year-old that meant a few more quid in my pocket as well as cheap fags, sweets and chocolate, which I thought was great at the time. There was a lad that I worked there with, Andrew Whetstone, who was a few years older than me and had a bit of a spiky quiff haircut going on. That didn't mean anything to start with but once we got to know each other we found some crossover in the music we both liked, and the inevitable record lending took place. This is where he introduced me to a new type of music. It was raw, energetic, a bit weird sometimes frankly and sounded like punked up rockabilly. The people that bought these records often wore flat top haircuts that were shaved short on the back and sides with the flat top bleached blonde then formed into gravity defying styles, vaguely resembling a teddy boy's quiff after he had stuck his fingers into an electrical plug socket to see what would happen. They might also wear checked shirts, big boots or vividly coloured T-shirts with a comical rat or a zombie type character on it. That was psychobilly.

Pyschobilly was fun, think wacky haircuts, a crazy style of "dancing" that was all elbows and fists, and onstage snakebite drinking competitions if you went to a King Kurt gig, from where you could also expect to leave the venue covered in flour and eggs or some other unknown noxious substances. You could hear a rockabilly influence in the music of bands like Guana Batz and Demented Are Go, if you imagined Carl Perkins on speed, but it could also be as intimidating as hell.

Only the Meteors were pure psychobilly, so they claimed, and I for one wasn't going to argue with the frontman P. Paul Fenech. To see them in full flow at The Klubfoot psychobilly nights, held at the Clarendon Hotel in Hammersmith, really was something else. The place was scary, and I've seen Fenech take a swing at someone in the crowd with his guitar at a gig there, maybe they looked at him the wrong way?

At a Sea Cadet Hall gig with friends, around 1987 – I'm 5th from left

Their followers, the Wreckin' Crew, would ensure that if you were going down the front at a gig and you survived the experience, you wouldn't forget it in a long time. The modern day mosh pit has nothing on The Wreckin' Crew, they were as hard as nails and controlled the "dance floor," they would decide if you could stay, and you'd know in no uncertain terms if you weren't welcome. It may have been testosterone fuelled bravado and a caveman way of proving yourself against your peers, but in a strange way it was welcoming too. If you were brave enough to go down the front and you fell, they wouldn't kick you while you were down but grab you and drag you back up to standing so that they could keep pummelling the life out of you for the rest of the set. Great Fun!

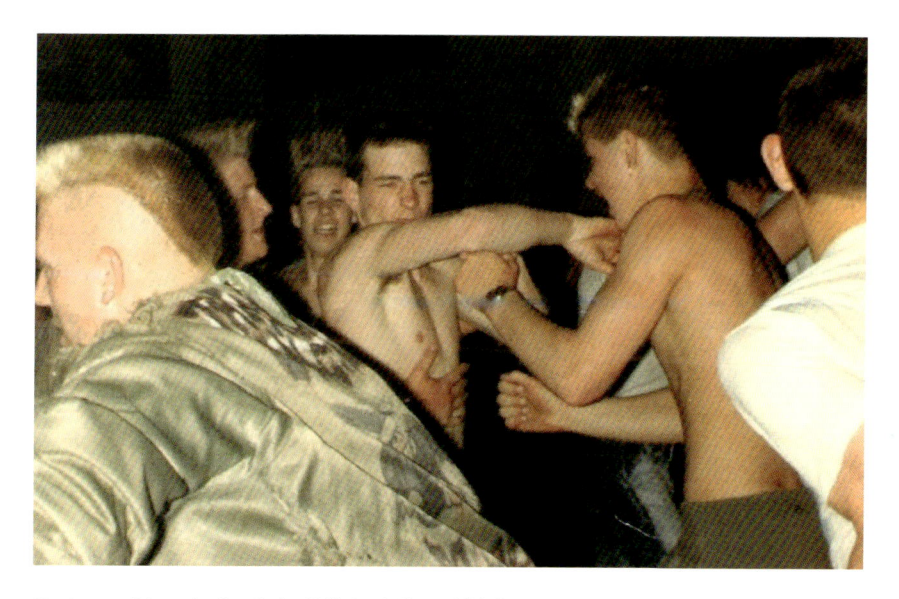

Getting stuck in at the Sea Cadet Hall gig. Spike Judd (left), Dave Russell (2nd left) and me (2nd right)

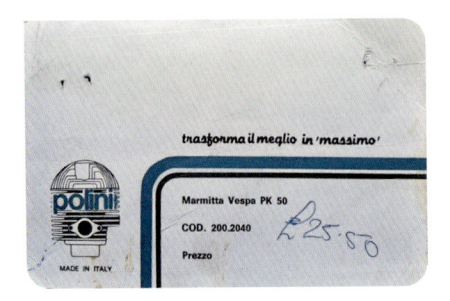

Vespa brochure cover and exhaust package label

THE CAT CLUB

The Guildhall, Cambridge

Held in the Small Hall, entrance opposite Chelsea Girl.

KING KURT

SAT 21st DEC

TICKETS £3·50

8:00pm – 11:00pm LICENSED BAR

Tickets available from:
Andy's Records, Mill Road. Tel: 61038.
The Beat Goes On, Regent Street. Tel: 66544.
The Box Office, Central Library, Lion Yard. Tel: 357851.

Promoted by Cambridge City Council.

LIVE MUSIC

Designed by Ted Koehorst of Trevor Vincent Graphics

At my new job, one of the sales reps that would visit was an old fella called Ray. He was only about 35 or 40 years old but to the 16-year-old me he was an old fella. My view of him changed though when he caught sight of my scooter, which dragged him straight back to memories of his youth. "Whose Vespa is that?" he asked one day. When I told him it was mine, I got the full "I used to be a mod, had a GS160! Went to Clacton and everything." I couldn't believe it, I was talking to a real, kosher sixties mod, he might even be in one of the photos in the Richard Barnes book that I had spent hours gawping at. He talked about his scooters that, like mine, had the crash bars and Florida bars bolted on, about the clothes he wore and the US Army fishtail parka with its fur lined hood. He even recalled how a few years earlier he was watching telly with his family when his daughter cried out "Dad look, you're on the telly!", and there he saw himself, in a black and white film shot at one of the Bank Holiday gatherings where hundreds of other mods on their scooters had descended on a coastal resort for the weekend. A real "petty little hoodlum, a sawdust Caesar," as a Margate magistrate described these young visitors that seemed to be intent on causing trouble and mayhem in the sleepy English seaside towns of the 1960s. But now he was just a normal bloke admiring MY scooter, reliving HIS youth and I really could not imagine him violently crashing a deck chair down on some poor rocker's head, but you never can tell.

That was all great and fascinating to hear and I loved it, but it was going back in time and even though I loved all the history, the music and all the connections that there were with Vespas and Lambrettas, that was 20 years previous, before I was even born, a lifetime away. It was when Dad had already put his Beatle suit towards the back of the wardrobe, was courting Mum and would soon ask the army for special leave so that he could make an honest woman of her. What I needed was something up to date and relevant, that I could immerse myself in, finding a place to fit in and make it my world, I just didn't know it yet.

No one else I knew so far was into scooters and I did not really think that there was much to do that involved them, apart from riding around the local area. The Bank Holiday gatherings of mods and their scooters in the sixties were in the past and, as far as I knew, did not happen anymore. I also did not realise how something like psychobilly would connect with

Heading home, my view from the family car

scooters until later on. But, earlier that year, when my mum, dad, brother, sister and I were returning from a visit to see family in Liverpool, I would see groups of scooters and their riders huddled round the fuel pumps at petrol stations or parked up in large groups at motorway service areas having a smoke and a break from where they had been riding to or from. This was not near the coast, and they weren't the mods that I had seen in my book or on record sleeves. They generally didn't have their scooters decked out in all the shiny bolt on adornments that I would expect them to have if they were mods and where they had been or what they had been doing I really did not know, and I also didn't know anyone that could tell me.

A NEW ENGLAND

My first winter on a scooter saw me riding through wind, rain and snow and experiencing the joys of mud and slime left by farmer's tractors and inclement weather. Combining those elements with the inferior quality of Swallow branded white wall tyres and my inexperience, led to a steep learning curve. It was one thing riding through mud on a push bike, but now having an engine to help get me into trouble and tyres that would give the impression of riding on an ice rink if conditions were not favourable, kept my nerves on edge and quickly built my character. Common sense saw me investing in some gloves, a scarf, and a full face fibreglass crash helmet for winter weather protection but, as is still the case 40 years later, if you want quality, you pay the money. Back then I didn't have the money, and the quality wasn't there either, so I made the best of a bad job and when I got home, I'd head straight to the living room to warm up in front of the Robinson Willey gas fire hoping my Jam stage shoes and gloves would dry out in time for the return journey to work the next day!

Early in the new year of 1985 having enjoyed my first six months on a scooter, I then experienced the reality and risk of riding a two wheeled vehicle on the road. Heading home from work one night it was dark, and a mixture of rain and sleet was making things difficult. I had my scarf covering my mouth and nose, the visor is down on my crash helmet and the rain is creating a starlight effect through it from the headlights of the oncoming traffic. Visibility is poor in these wet conditions, the contrast between road, kerb and pavement is non-existent and the weak scooter headlight doesn't help in picking out the tricky features in the road surface that make riding more difficult on two wheels compared to four. I drop my speed trying to choose the best and safest line to take, avoiding the slippery manhole covers and dodgy road surfaces, whilst trying not to look directly into the dazzling headlights of the oncoming cars and steamed up buses heading home in the rush hour.

Even now, with many miles on my scootering clock, these conditions are still treacherous, and experience needs to be combined with a sense of self-preservation and a bit of luck to safely and successfully complete a journey. However, that night I was still building my experience and my luck was low. I gripped the handlebars, and my knees were tucked in behind the legshields trying to keep dry, my head is tucked down slightly into the rain and sleet while I peer ahead trying to find my way in the dark. I looked up and briefly glimpsed a solitary car parked next to the kerb. An Austin Princess, with no parking lights on to warn me of its presence, sat there benignly and claimed a victim. In a split second I'd seen the car and dragged the handlebars to the right but still crunched into its rear wing, experiencing for the first time that sickening sound of a scooter thudding into metal, crumpling the bodywork. The scooter stayed where it was, I was catapulted over the handlebars onto the tarmac, thankfully avoiding any further collision with the oncoming traffic. Dazed and wondering what the hell had happened; I stood up, got my bearings, and then looked back at my pride and joy. It didn't look good, the legshields were dented, the mudguard squashed, and the crash bars formed into new shapes. And the one thing I took away from all of this? It was a painful lesson, but this is where I found out… crash bars are of no bloody use in a crash!

So that was it, my first scooter, written off by the insurance company and now only a memory. I have no pictures of it, but it is still sharp in my mind's eye. A few years later I made a day visit to one of the Lowestoft mod rallies with mates and have two abiding memories. One was of being given a look of absolute disgust by one of the attendant mods because, shock horror, I was dressed in a skinhead style at a mod Rally, while the other was noticing a Vespa PK parked up and recognising its number plate as being from my first scooter. It was like seeing a long-lost friend and I can only assume that the insurance company sold it as a write off before it was fixed up and made roadworthy once more.

Carrying out a DVLA vehicle history search on their website as I write this, I can see that it was last taxed in 1996 but also that a V5 logbook was issued as recently as 2019. So, it is still out there somewhere. I'd like to think that it now sports race paintwork, a tuned engine and is being thrashed round a track somewhere, you never know. Now scooterless, I was reduced to cycling to work again and using the bus until I was able to get another. It was also worth waiting a couple of months until I was 17 and able to move up to the dizzying heights of a 125cc machine. It was tough and certainly would not be the last time I was off the road for a while.

One day, I had taken the bus into town and was in the Cambridge branch of Our Price Records looking for some new music to buy. As I was flicking through the racks of vinyl an older lad who I didn't know, nodded his head in acknowledgement and asked if I had a scooter. It was like making contact with someone from another planet but who spoke the same language as me. He was dressed in Dr Marten's boots, army green combat trousers, a proper MA1 flight jacket and had a crew cut. He told me his name was Zom, short for Zombie. I never asked him why he was given that name, probably best not to. Thinking back on it, I imagine his mum poking her head out of the back door of their house and bellowing out, "Zombie, come and get your tea!" because she just could not bring herself to call him Zom, as everyone knows mums always call their child by their full name.

Zom asked me all the usual questions; what did I ride, where was I from, and was I going to the scooter run at Morecambe? Going? I was now, scooter or no scooter! My geographical knowledge of the UK has been built up by riding my scooter around the country to attend scooter rallies, or scooter runs as they were often called then, custom shows and other similar events. I probably didn't even know where Morecambe was back then, but I was soon to find out. Without the luxury of today's satnav systems or mobile phones, the most popular choice of finding your way to a scooter run back then, apart from following the signs that proclaimed "A1 and the North", was with the legendary Little Chef Road Map, supplied by the roadside café chain whose staff must have dreaded the hordes of scooterists that would invade their establishments for a fry up breakfast, or to indulge in a serving of pancakes and ice cream. The scooterboys and girls from the 1980s were not renowned for their sophisticated palate. The Little Chef map was not highly detailed, being a leaflet that unfolded to show a map of the entire United Kingdom, with main roads, major towns, cities and of course, the entire network of Little Chefs. Navigating from one end of the country to the other using this humble item was a big ask, but with it you did at least stand a chance of arriving at your destination and is now fondly remembered by the many that were there. If you were lucky (?), you might have an AA route map that your dad had ordered for you but wouldn't actually be used due to its impracticalities on a scooter. Imagine firstly, a ream of printed pages with instructions like: follow the High Street for 0.5 mile, turn right at the T-Junction onto Church Road, follow the road for

0.5 mile, turn right at the T-Junction onto Airport Way for 0.75 mile, at the roundabout take the 2nd exit onto the A1303 towards Newmarket, follow for 1 mile, at the roundabout take the 1st exit… and that was just to get out of the village! Secondly, imagine that ream of paperwork somehow fixed to a scooter's handlebars or toolbox door whilst still being able to turn the pages at regular intervals and in the typical weather of an English bank holiday, infamously wet and windy. It just wasn't going to happen, Little Chef Road Map for the masses it was then.

So now I knew there was a scooter run taking place, I knew where and I knew when. I have heard of scooterists travelling long distances to a distant seaside town on a Vespa PK50 or a Vespa 50 special (a truly iconic scooter for any self-respecting 16-year-old), only to have to turn around pretty much on arrival, and then head home if there was to be any chance of getting back in time for work on the Monday morning. I no longer had that option though, so some lateral thinking was needed if I was to attend my first National Scooter Rally.

A plan was hatched a lot easier than expected. I found out that Morecambe isn't that far from Mum and Dad's home city of Liverpool. As a kid, the family would regularly travel up to see relations that still lived there. I had ducked out of the last couple of trips as I was now old enough to stay at home on my own and let's face it, how many parents would rather leave a surly 16-year-old at home than endure a whole weekend with them. But, for one more trip I would honour them with my presence when they drove north for the Easter weekend of 1985. So that was my transport sorted as far north as Liverpool. From there I caught a train from Lime Street Station that would get me to Morecambe after changing trains en route. Now I know I was going to a scooter rally on a train and that is sacrilege to some, but this was a whole new world I was entering, and I needed to see what was involved sooner rather than later. Knowing me though, if I hadn't already totalled my first scooter in that crash, I may well have given the 250 mile trip at least a thought, in my naivety.

As it turned out, I wasn't the only one taking the train up to Morecambe. On the first leg there was a handful of people with the same idea but, when I changed trains and got on to the second, I was completely and utterly bowled over by what I saw. There were only two or three carriages, but they were rammed to the gunnels with youngsters dressed in army greens and flight jackets covered in patches; skinheads wearing Crombie coats and neck tattoos, mod girls with bob haircuts, pyschobillies with huge flat tops and goths wearing leather jackets. I stepped through the doors wondering whether it was actually a good idea after all. The atmosphere was electric, most people knew what they were doing and looking back were buzzing for the first scooter run of the new season, but it was also as scary as hell. What would happen if I caught the eye of the mean looking skinhead? Would he give me "the evils" or growl the classic line at me from back then of "Wot you looking at!" to which I would have bravely answered by lighting up bright red and stuttering "Nothing" in return, before turning away in fear of my life. The 1980s felt oppressive and violent as a kid. The various tribal subcultures that teenagers aligned themselves with were very easily identified by clothes and haircuts and they tended to only welcome others in that looked as they did. They would often clash with other groups outside the school gates, music gigs or football matches. As a young mod, I had experienced casuals giving me grief in a local shopping centre, bikers ride past me on my scooter giving me a nazi salute and smoothies hurl abuse at me from the safety of their car. But there, on that train, there were people who the red top newspapers would call the "scum of the earth" and who you would expect to tear each other apart as soon as look at each other. I had never seen anything like it, but all was good. I kept myself to myself, taking it all in until we arrived at Morecambe. Everyone filed off the train and walked along the platform in a large group full of anticipation of the rally. I dread to think what was going through the ticket collector's mind as we continued through the barriers out of the Victorian built railway station and onto the street.

There were scooters everywhere and of course they were surrounded by the people who had ridden them there. Lambrettas and Vespas together, all the different models, some old some new. Immaculately painted scooters in all the colours imaginable lining the kerb, decorated with murals and sign written panels. Brand new Vespa PXs stood next to older Lambretta GPs sparkling in their metal flake paint with the legend "AF Rayspeed Extra S-Type" emblazoned on their side panels, along with scruffy scooters, bodywork removed, and machines that looked like motorcycle choppers but with small wheels. What was going on? This was nothing like I expected, all my preconceptions built up from the likes of Quadrophenia and The Jam were there, in small amounts, but not the blanket coverage that I was expecting. It was such a mix, a mishmash of so many other styles and influences and I would capture many of the different scooters and styles on my camera along the way, so that I could gaze over the developed photographs when I was back at home.

A Lambretta GP in the iconic AF Rayspeed Extra "S" Type livery

Walking along the Morecambe sea front; past the arcades, cafés and chip shops facing out onto the bay, was not easy, partly due to the holiday makers trying to enjoy their bank holiday but mainly down to the vast number of people there for the scooters, and they all were having the time of their lives. Parked along the kerb was scooter after scooter, stretching on and on, the air was full of the noise and smell of these machines being constantly ridden up and down the seafront. In front of bed and breakfast hotels, scooters were squeezed into any available parking space possible and looked like they would not be moved for the weekend. Walking passed the local pubs I could see why; they were full of scooterists who, it turns out, love a good drink. If there wasn't room inside, they just spilled out onto the pavement outside; drinking, smoking, and enjoying themselves. This carried on all along the sea front, down into the side streets and wherever else I looked. I can't remember now what I wore, jeans maybe Sta-prest with a Fred Perry T-shirt and either a monkey jacket or a cheap flight jacket but either way I seemed to fit in, no one jostled me or hurled abuse at me. Things were looking alright.

At some point, I got talking to a few Welsh scooterists. A year or two older than me I would have said and very welcoming. They seemed to recognise the look of a new arrival and it felt like they had an idea of what they were doing, so the offer to tag along was welcome and we all headed along to the campsite. Now, when I say campsite do not imagine nicely tended lawns with serviced shower blocks and a playground for the kids, think more along the lines of a huge, grassed area, maybe common land, looking down onto the sea and within sight of the Heysham Nuclear Power Station, at least the bathing water would be warm! Scooterists back then were not seen as money making opportunities to be welcomed with open arms. They were often met with signs stating "No Scooterists" outside pubs, lodgings, and campsites. Rally campsites were often on what looked like farmer's fields, sometimes car parks or waste land, whatever the local council gave us or whatever the organisers were able to arrange. I cannot remember now what I had planned for my overnight stay in Morecambe, if anything, but the site did not look particularly welcoming considering that all I had with me was what I stood in; no sleeping bag, tent or even a toothbrush. I dread to think where I told Mum and Dad I was staying overnight, different times.

The Morecambe campsite with the nuclear power station in the background

Wandering around the camp site I continued to be amazed at the many assorted styles of scooters. There were stalls with shiny scooter parts for sale as well as records and patches, people milling about drinking, chatting, and like me, taking in all the sights and sounds. Northern soul tunes were played over a PA sound system loud enough to be heard over the sound of two stroke engines buzzing around the site. I bought my first northern soul single there, "I Surrender" by Eddie Holman backed with "Just One More Chance" by The Patrick Bradley, and "I Can't Escape from You" by Richie Adams, in a black, white, and red paper sleeve on the Kent reissue label. I didn't know the tunes, being more familiar with the well-known Tamla Motown record label than the many northern soul songs I would hear in the future, but it was a low-risk punt, probably only costing

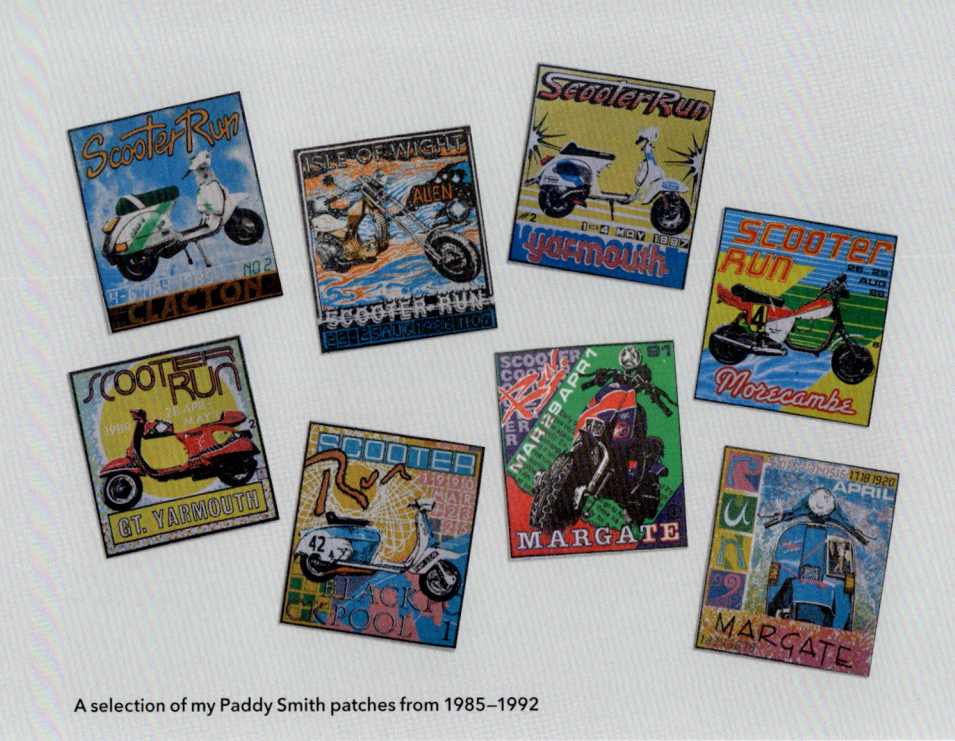

A selection of my Paddy Smith patches from 1985–1992

a couple of quid, and as it turned out, was a good introduction to this style of music and great to dance to. Northern soul has been a big part of the scooter scene for some time, and you can't avoid it at most rallies and events, which is great if you're a fan. I know many people don't like it, but I grew to really enjoy the tunes and would occasionally strut my stuff on the dance floor after a couple of shandies to the classic four to the floor beat that it is renowned for.

Two other first purchases for me from the campsite, which in the future I wouldn't leave for home without, were the rally T-shirt and rally patch. My first T-shirt was grey with ON THE RUN printed in red and Vespa, Lambretta and 1985 in blue in a block design. I can't remember who printed the patch, but it was a circular design reading NATIONAL SCOOTER RALLY and MORECAMBE – EASTER – APRIL 5.6.7.8 above an image of a Lambretta chopper with extended forks. The patches were a memento of the rally and collecting them would later become a record of attending a particular rally, with many scooterists covering their jackets and sometimes trousers with them. I hadn't ridden to this rally nor would I to my second a month later at Clacton, but the experience was unforgettable and from then onwards, having a roadworthy scooter to ride to a rally would always be the aim, or at the very least, getting a lift on a mate's scooter if I didn't.

The most highly regarded scooter rally patch was the Paddy or Paddy Smith, as it was known. Only available to be bought from the maker, no prizes for guessing his name, on the rally itself. Paddy Smith and his helpers would run a stall on the campsite where one of these legendary patches could be bought, and it would become the first place to visit on site to ensure a confirmed purchase. Often people would buy two patches, one for their jacket and one as a keepsake. They were prized and a full season of nine rallies would make an impressive block of patches on the back of any jacket. Ownership of one these patches was (generally) seen as proof of rally attendance, due to Paddy destroying any unsold patches straight after the rally, which other patch makers could not claim.

The Welsh lads were talking of an all-nighter that was taking place. This would be the main organised event of the rally, playing scooter orientated music through the night, including a lot of northern soul. A big plus of these all-nighters was that if you were there throughout then you wouldn't be sleeping in a cold, cramped or wet tent next to the sea. Remember, this was Morecambe over a bank holiday weekend, not a great harbinger of good weather. Tickets were bought and we then walked back in the direction of the main town. Somewhere along the way I started to get cold feet, decided to give the all-nighter a miss and got myself separated from the others. If any of the Welsh lads from back then recognise themselves, thanks for taking me under your wing for that short bit of time and apologies for ducking out without an explanation or a goodbye. I then wandered back to the railway station, taking more photos of the many different scooters, before catching a train back to Lime Street and my lift home in the car to Cambridge.

The effect this first rally had on me was massive and profound. Like many others at the time, I went to the rally a young mod, having dressed both myself and my scooter in the defining way of that youth subculture. Returning home, I no longer felt shackled to have to dress in just one way, listen to a specific genre of music or to ride a certain style of scooter, I had finally arrived at a place where I felt comfortable and where I didn't have to fit in to fit in. Yes, there were looks that were common on the rallies; mod, skinhead, scooterboy, pyschobilly and so on, but even if you weren't one of those you were still included and part of the scooter scene if you rode a scooter.

Soon after, on Saturday the 13th of July 1985, The Style Council followed Status Quo onto the stage at Wembley Stadium at the Live Aid concert, also on that day I fully ditched my mod style clothes for the more practical garb of the scooterboy. At the local army surplus store, I bought my first pair of Dr Martens AirWair boots, army green combat trousers and a proper MA1 flight jacket. I had gone to Morecambe a mod but had most definitely returned as a scooterboy, and whatever I wanted that to be.

SUSPECT DEVICE

This new world enthralled me, it gave me direction and provided a steep learning curve, both about the scene and the scooters. Shortly after Morecambe, my mate Jason and I caught a coach and headed to Clacton and the next National Scooter Rally, held over the Mayday bank holiday weekend. Jason Hughes was a close friend from the village and a couple of years younger than me. We had a lot in common through music, but I don't recall that he was thinking of getting into the scooter scene at that time. If he wasn't, Clacton would have given him a push in that direction as he did later buy a Vespa, another PK50S. One time I gave him a lift on it due to him being out of riding action with a leg injury. I had my full licence by then so no major problem there you'd think, but this particular injury meant he was on crutches and needed to carry them for when we arrived at our destination. Picture the scene, an already underpowered Vespa scooter, two-up with the passenger (Jason) trying not to disrupt the scooter's balance due to his discomfort and the crutches he was carrying, and the rider (me) wondering why the scooter was suddenly and violently squirming it's way around a busy roundabout, before realising that the rear tyre was massively under inflated. Somehow, we kept upright and alive. Whether this situation was down to a puncture or poor maintenance

I don't remember, but it was close and was one of the many little tales that would be retold over the years in a pub or on a rally.

Clacton was very much like Morecambe. We wandered the sea front and the campsite in awe of all the scooters on display, soaking up all the new wonders whilst snapping away furiously with our little instamatic cameras. Unlike Morecambe, we did however make the all-nighter, not the whole night though as we were staying with the family of Jason's cousin in the town so needed to get back to our kind hosts at a respectable time to avoid the wrath of Jason's parents on our return. We were scooterboys in training, but we still had rules to follow, and I would have to wait till the following year, 1986, before I could fully immerse myself in the joys of riding to, and camping at, a scooter rally. In the meantime, I needed another scooter.

Back then the local newspaper had a motorcycles and scooters for sale section in the classified ads. This is where I found my next scooter, a Vespa 150 Super. Not a classic in hindsight with its 8" wheels and dulled light blue paintwork. It lacked the smooth and sultry curves of the earlier GS model I had seen in the Mods! book, but it most definitely caught my eye, and after a phone call to the seller, plans were made to borrow one of the work's vans, with a work colleague driving it, to go to view the scooter and hopefully bring it home. We headed over to meet the seller, all was well, and I handed over the £25 being asked for. Bearing in mind I had no mechanical knowledge of an internal combustion engine prior my PK50 and no experience of buying a second-hand scooter at that point, I was easily dazzled in my enthusiasm for obtaining another scooter. The seller seemed decent enough, the scooter was all in one piece, it started, ran and all the electrics (lights and horn) worked as needed. I eagerly handed over the grand sum of £25, loaded the scooter into the van and headed off home.

The scooter's engine size was 150cc, but my provisional licence only entitled me to ride up to a 125cc displaying learner's L-Plates. In his parental role of keeping me legal and alive, Dad insisted that if I wanted to ride this machine it needed to have a 125cc engine. This is where I started to gain my mechanical knowledge. Many years later I am happy to strip my scooter's engine down to a collection of parts and then repair and replace

Aged 16, on the Vespa 150 Super MOT failure

parts as necessary before rebuilding it, but back then I was clueless as to what was needed to alter, maintain, and keep a scooter running. This is where the learning began. After speaking to one of the local scooter shops as to how to reduce the engine's capacity to make it learner legal, a new 125cc top end (consisting of a barrel, piston, and cylinder head) was ordered. The idea was a simple one, remove the old top end and replace it with the new one, at two or three times the original cost of the scooter it has to be said. This was to become a recurring theme over the years, and I dare to think a) how much money I have spent on scooters over the years and b) how much of that money was wasted!

Luckily, I knew how to use a spanner and screwdriver, and of course a hammer, from fixing my push bikes and had been studying an old copy of a Haynes manual for the Vespa. The operation took place in the back garden. I remember removing the necessary parts, lifting off the cylinder barrel and prising the securing clips away from the piston, removing the old piston from the con rod and fitting the new one. Doing this job requires gaskets of the correct thickness, sealant to ensure a patent seal with no leakages as well as tolerances set to the correct measurements and jetting changes to the carburettor to ensure an effective and reliable engine. The gaskets and sealant help to seal the join between two components against air leaks. These leaks are the arch enemy of a two-stroke engine and can easily cause fatal damage to the piston and cylinder bore, cutting a journey short and requiring major mechanical intervention to repair. I didn't appreciate all the technicalities and implications of this at the time and so, using my ingenuity, I cut a couple of gaskets from a cereal box to sandwich between the engine casing, cylinder and cylinder head. It seemed like a clever idea at the time. Years later I now realise the importance of a well put together engine, but back then a Cornflake packet and a straight swap of parts did the job. The engine amazingly started after rebuilding it and on the sly, when Mum and Dad were at work, I would push the scooter the half mile or so up to the rec road for a test ride, the scooter not yet having an MOT. Those were the days of neighbours stitching you up to parents for scrumping fruit from their garden, so daring to ride your scooter on the road illegally ran a significant risk with their watchful eyes, and I needed to keep Dad on my side rather than make trouble for myself. It was also when I tasted petrol for the first time, having persuaded a mate to let me syphon off some petrol from his moped when my scooter ran out of petrol. Horrible stuff and I sometimes wonder how I made it to adulthood in one piece.

With the scooter's engine downsized, it was booked in for an MOT, ridden there and dropped off for the formality of the necessary checks. What could go wrong? It was a basic little machine, the brakes braked, the lights came on and went off when asked to, there were no indicators to worry about and the horn performed a ridiculous but satisfactory noise that resembled a duck's fart. Again, what could go wrong? Well, a bloody big hole out of sight and underneath the floorboards is what could and did go wrong. This is where I really started climbing the steep learning curve that I mentioned earlier. A significant patch of a structural part of the steel frame had rusted through, the MOT tester looked like he genuinely felt my pain as he leaned the scooter over to show me the damage causing the failure. These days, if buying an old Vespa, I wouldn't even start the scooter's engine up without checking the underside area of the frame for that common damage. It was fixable, but back then I didn't have any idea where or how to get the frame repaired and the shop couldn't help, so sadly the scooter was ridden home and parked up. It was never ridden legally on the road after that, never mind to a scooter rally and where it ended up is now lost in the dark recesses of my memory.

LAST GOODBYE

In the 1980s, the scooter scene felt different to other subcultures, much more open and accepting. It was easy to interact with other scooterists because there was always something to talk about; Had you been to the last rally? Were you going to the next one? What scooter did you ride? Did you belong to a club? You could share tales of scooter mishaps or of a particularly arduous ride to a rally. Whether you had a skinhead crop, a flat top or a wedge haircut, if you had a jacket clustered with rally patches, a crash helmet or wore some scooter badges and rode a scooter, it was not difficult to strike up a conversation. A lot of the other teenage tribes would all look the same. Because they were mates and because there is a need to be accepted by your peers at that time in life, they would dress like each other, always go to the same pub and listen to the same music. Their connections would be the experiences they shared together in their hometown and their jokes would be understood by that group but probably not by outsiders. Scooter clubs would have their in-jokes and probably one person that everyone ridiculed, but their world and their experiences extended far beyond the city ring road and their acquaintances were spread around the country. Having met them once in an obscure pub in an English seaside town it would be likely to meet them at another rally in another town another time.

The scooter scene was growing and expanding for me, in the same way that a cell divides and multiplies, constantly changing and evolving, so meeting one new person would inevitably introduce me to a couple more. Some of the kids below me at school could now be seen walking around wearing parkas and then not long after they would be riding a Vespa PK or 50 Special. As with anyone looking for a safe environment, these new scooter riders would group together and bring friends into the group who either had or liked scooters and they would become part of the growing group. This is what happened where I lived and before long there was a group of us that would congregate together and then buzz around local villages on our scooters. We spent a period of our lives together that could never be recreated, long before mortgages, before starting our own nuclear families, before responsibilities and pension plans. A mixed bunch, sharing the love of scooters but who would eventually scatter around the country, finding their own way in the world.

I knew Jason Hughes and Dwain Smith from primary school onwards, both a couple of years younger. Jason got into scooters and the national rallies after visiting Clacton with me, and we would be part of the same larger scooter crowd in Cambridge in the following years, drinking together and going to the same rallies and gigs. He was my best man when I got married but as often happens, life takes you in different directions and you lose contact. He has lived down on the south coast now for longer than he has not, playing guitar in various local bands. I had the pleasure of bumping into him some years ago. Over a beer the conversation did not take long to turn to scooters and finding out that he still had his old Lambretta in the shed at his parent's house, a plan was made to get it back

With Jason Hughes (centre) and David Childs (right). Margate 2007

on the road for him. Sadly, it was in a bad way and in need of a full rebuild. Plan B was hatched, and I took on the project of restoring the scooter to its former glory for him, bringing back memories from long ago and the trips that were made on it. It was a satisfying day when he collected the finished SX200 from me some months later and around that time, along with another mate David Childs, we would drag him along to one more Margate rally, for old time's sake. As with many old friends who only see each other once in a blue moon, we would soon get back on track with the three of us talking and laughing about days passed, while drinking and dancing through the night before heading home.

Dwain was a very different person, a cheeky little sod at times but a good lad and I had pretty much grown up with both him and Jason, hanging around on street corners, bunking round his house in the long school holidays when his mum and dad were at work and sneaking gulps of booze with him from their drinks cabinet without them knowing (at least I don't think they knew!). Dwain got himself a little run down Vespa 50 Special which, with his dad Colin's help, they had resprayed black with gold trim, fitted a little sports seat, and slipped in a larger 125cc engine. It turned out to be a tidy little scooter and quite nippy too. In 1987 we would ride down to the Isle of Wight together, him on his 50 Special and me on my Vespa Primavera 125.

Riding a scooter or a motorbike involves an amount of risk, many people think they are dangerous machines, and some people do not take up riding because of this. Many people, like me, love to ride and accept the risk but do our best to keep that risk at an acceptable level. If you have ridden for long enough, you may have experienced the loss of a friend in an accident or a crash. Dwain was that person for me. When he was 17 years old, Dwain had moved onto a Lambretta GP which he was riding when he was sadly killed in a collision caused by a car driver who was in too much of a rush. I have never experienced the emotions I felt when, on a Saturday morning, I knocked on his house door to check that it was not him that was involved in the accident the previous evening. Sarah, his sister, answered the door and seeing me, called their Nan to come and speak to me. I knew then that I would not be seeing Dwain again.

Gathering for Dwain's funeral

With Dwain (left) and his Vespa 50 Special

Soon after, I approached Dwain's parents, Colin and Jenny, for permission to organise a procession of scooters to travel to the church where he was to be buried. Knowing a lot more people in the scooter scene by that time, we had between 20 and 30 scooters taking part on the day. Anticipating this, I had arranged a police motorcycle outrider to escort us through the centre of Cambridge, preventing the group from being split up. We caused quite a sight, made the local newspaper, and gave Dwain a great send off. Where he was laid to rest was in a village some way outside of Cambridge. The weather was typical for that time of year in the Fens of Cambridgeshire; bitterly cold, damp, grey and dreary, almost Dickensian and befitting the occasion.

That was November 1987. Over the years I kept in touch and would occasionally visit Colin, Jenny and Sarah. Many years later I asked what had happened to the little 50 Special, they told me that it had sat under a tarpaulin for a long time in the back garden. One day they eventually decided to uncover it to decide what to do with it. Sadly, it had the all too common rust under the floorboards that can attack a Vespa. The frame had collapsed in on itself and it ended up being take to the tip as scrap. I cannot even begin to imagine the heartbreak that they both must have felt at that moment.

ANGLEGRINDER BLUES

Having spent my early teenage years gathering on street corners, hanging around bus shelters and smoking illicit cigarettes with school mates, I now found I was doing the same thing but with a different crowd of friends. We hadn't got into frequenting pubs yet, so the streets were where we still socialised. It did not help that when one of us did try to buy an underage drink from our local pub, the landlord, having known us all since we were young kids, would stop that rite of passage, barring us until we were of legal age. The scooters we rode were small frame Vespas or nondescript Lambrettas. At that time cheap Italian scooters could be picked up quite often and easily from old fellas that did not feel the need any longer to expose themselves to the elements on an old scooter. After the Vespa Super failed its MOT, I picked up an Italian Lambretta SX150 in bits with the intention of rebuilding it into a complete machine, ever the optimist. I remember extraordinarily little of this scooter apart from some over ambitious ideas with my limited finances and skills. With some tips from a friend, I did have a go at spray painting the side panels a nice metallic deep red. I seem to recall this going quite well but have no idea what happened to it after that.

Following that, I heard about a scooter that was being sold in the next village that sounded promising. An Italian DL125 in purple. Now I was getting somewhere, it was being sold by one of the afore-mentioned old fellas. It was complete; working, had all its bodywork and in 15 years had probably only been ridden at sedate speeds within the borders of Cambridgeshire by "one careful owner", and was for sale at the bargain price of £150. He was happy to relieve me of the asking price, so I don't think the seller was too sentimental about handing his precious machine over to a young upstart with a funny haircut, which was just as well as within a couple of weeks I had been pulled over by a local village copper for exceeding the speed limit on the way to work, and soon after that the piston disintegrated on me while riding. With my recently gained experience, that wasn't too much of a problem though. A new piston was sourced and fitted before soon being mobile again. For some reason, this scooter was badged as a DL which in theory meant it was an Italian market scooter, as the British market were sold the same model but badged up as a Grand Prix or GP. The Lambretta DL/GP has always been my favourite of the Lambrettas having seen them properly for the first time at Morecambe. The Bertone designed bodywork is smooth and modern, in fact it still looks fresh over 50 years later and looks fast just standing still, this is also the model I have been riding for well over 10 years now. Along with the later Vespa PX, it was the foundation of thousands of rally going machines from the early 1970s in the northern scooter scene, through the peak times of the national rallies in the 1980s. On the custom scene it became ubiquitous, often due to the expansive areas of flat and smooth bodywork it had, making it easy for a spray gun artist to work their magic on with race replica paintwork, metalflake or as a muralled mobile work of art. It was around this time that I first met older Cambridge scooterboy Andy Hawes on his Lambretta GP Death in the Afternoon, a tastily muralled scooter on the theme of Spanish Bull Fighting. He was a larger than life gentle giant with an infectious giggle that intensified tenfold after indulging in one or two herbal cigarettes.

Andy Hawes fixing one of his scooters

With Steve Brown (left) and Tom Quigley (right)

He built a few tasty scooters, starting off with a well-known rally scooter of the early 1980s called The Legend Lives On, as well as a bright yellow cutdown Lambretta street racer with Lambretta Vega legshields called Little Lamb Bee, which was bought by a mate Tom Quigley, and finishing with the understated and classy Death in the Afternoon. Some years later this scooter would spend time on display at the Lambretta Preservation Museum in Devon. To know an older, rally experienced scooterboy with a custom machine at the time was nothing short of mind blowing to the young me.

Now having a proper scooter, my mind was set on using it to ride to at least one of the national rallies in 1986. Also, having seen more and more scooterists at gigs such as Spear of Destiny on their World Service Tour, The Guana Batz and King Kurt, and on return visits to the Klubfoot, I was loving the freedom to wear what I wanted to and have the haircut to match but still ride a scooter, such a difference to the constraints of being a mod. So, it was about that time that my run of the mill crewcut was grown out and replaced with a pyschobilly flat top. I gave my mum the fright of her life one Saturday afternoon with my latest look. I had been told to visit a traditional gents barber in Cambridge for the new hairstyle, and where, with my youthful features, I disappointingly never did get asked "Something for the weekend Sir?" It was where someone by the name of Boppo worked, who was probably responsible for the vast majority of rockabilly and psychobilly haircuts in the area. Getting home with the new flat top, and to finish it off, I set to work with a bottle of hydrogen peroxide bought from Boots. I was after the white blonde that I had seen sported by Billy Duffy of The Cult and Stan Stammers of Spear of Destiny. Mum's heart must have missed a beat when she walked into the living room, saw my new, more yellow than blonde, hair style and shrieked "What have you done?!" in the same way she would have if I had been a toddler and my dad had just cut off all the curly locks that I had at that age! Anyway, the deed was done and over time the flat top grew taller, it would be rebleached to the intended tone and paired with a leather biker jacket, army green combat trousers and 10 hole Dr Martens to achieve the child scaring (unintended but true) psycho-scooterbilly look, as termed by Spike Judd, one of the Cambridge psychobillies I was to meet and enjoy many a beer with. The child scaring episode took place one Saturday afternoon while I was walking through the Lion Yard shopping centre in Cambridge, and ironically within yards of where a small group of casuals had previously walked into me as a young mod, trying to intimidate me by one of them smashing his knee into my thigh to give me a dead leg purely because of the clothes I wore, mad. This time, as I was walking along minding my own business, I noticed two young kids of about eight years old walking towards me, eyes agog in awe of the sight of me and my scary haircut, who then suddenly split either side of me apparently in fear of their lives, despite me not being the fearsome person they thought I was. It is amazing how people are judged simply by looks alone (but we all do it) and my tall, spiked haircut, ear piercings, leather jacket and boots must have terrified those poor souls. Strangely enough though, I never met any more casuals who felt the need to try and menace me from around that time onwards.

The two magazines in circulation at that time, British Scooter Scene and Scootering, supplied the dates and locations of forthcoming rallies. These were published at the start of the year once the No 1s (representatives) of various scooter clubs around the country had met and agreed the details. This openness would soon change following future events, and information restricted with the aim of deterring certain factions of people from disrupting events dues to their dodgy political and racist views, but for now, information was easily obtained, and plans could be made for a whole rally season.

Great Yarmouth was listed to be the first rally of 1986, and I was counting the days down in anticipation. Not long before that though, Dwain had called round begging me to loan him the DL so that he could nip to the next village to see some mates. I refused and held out for some time as he badgered me on the doorstep of my house, but when he offered to fill up the tank with petrol and bring back a couple of packets of fags for me, well my arm was well and truly twisted. The keys were handed over and off he went. It was quite some time before he returned, and it soon became quite clear why he had been delayed. The little bugger had only been posing on my scooter in front of a girl he fancied, hormones have a lot to answer for at that age. He had been riding up and down the street, trying to pull the odd wheely in the hope of making a positive impression on the girl. An impression was made, not so much on the intended target but on an innocent concrete bollard at the side of the road. On one of his wheely attempts, he over cooked it and lost control, veering to the side and colliding with one of a row of bollards protecting some shop frontages. The bollards certainly fulfilled their purpose, and my scooter came off worst. The legshields were dented and creased while the kickstart return lug had been forced into the engine's side casing creating a big hole for the gearbox oil to pour out from. The scooter was unrideable, and Dwain had endured a shameful two-mile walk pushing my scooter back to explain everything to me. I'm sure some expletives would have been hurled in his direction and the fags owed to me would have increased in quantity, but it was not enough to break a friendship and now it's a fond memory of Dwain from long ago. It also meant that, once the work had been done, I would be riding to Great Yarmouth on a proper scooterboy cutdown after the damaged legshields had been removed, necessity being the mother of invention.

So, one morning in late March, another mate Carl Ireland and I set off for the Great Yarmouth national scooter rally. We were both dressed in army green combat trousers and MA1 flight jackets, Carl wore boxing boots, and I had Dr Martens, he had a mohawk haircut and there was I with my newly bleached flat top haircut, flattened very effectively by my crash helmet. This was very much a common look on the rallies but not the only one, however like the earlier child scaring incident, to Joe Public we must have looked a daunting prospect with the numbers that would invade a seaside town billowing two-stroke noise and fumes wherever we went. This time though, we had made some plans for accommodation. We each took a sleeping bag, mine being Dads old army issue one, with the intention of meeting up with mates and bunking in a tent that they had taken. We did meet up with them thankfully (I think?), but that must have been one of the most cramped and uncomfortable night's sleep I have ever experienced with us all squashed into such a small space. From Cambridge we had about 80 miles to travel to reach our destination and we should get there by early afternoon, or so we thought.

We set off, full of the excitement of riding to a rally for the first time, Carl on his Serveta Lynx that he had resprayed a light metallic blue, and me on the newly cutdown DL, when after a grand total of about two miles, and as we negotiated a roundabout to join the slip road to what was then the A45, Carl's scooter suffered its first puncture. Notice that I wrote first puncture not a puncture. The inner tube was replaced, and we were on our way again only to be bought to a stop very soon after with the same problem.

Carl Ireland fixing yet another puncture!

My cutdown DL125

Progress was painfully slow. It was a case of get puncture, stop, fix it, set off, repeat. We had used Carl's spare tube, a bicycle puncture repair kit and my spare before the decision was taken to leave Carl by the side of the road while I rode off in search of a new innertube. Luckily, I found a motorcycle shop in nearby Brandon where I could buy the correct size innertube and then head back to find Carl and continue our journey. I almost rode past him as a group of scooters that had stopped to help were gathered round him. At the last moment I saw him and pulled in towards the grass verge. Riding over some gravel as I braked, I came to a stop with a skid that sent stones flying everywhere and surprised everyone present, including me, but once the new innertube was fitted we were able to make decent progress, finally reaching our destination late in the afternoon.

We had completed all of 25 miles in the time the whole journey should have taken us, but eventually we were properly underway and heading for the seaside. Nine hours and thirty minutes after setting off, we eventually arrived at St Nicks car park in Great Yarmouth where the rally was based, giving an average speed of less than 10 miles per hour. The journey was laughable in hindsight but left us with fantastic memories of a vastly different time in life that I wouldn't change for anything.

At this time, scooter rallies often had bands and artists playing at nighttime dos. People like Edwin Starr, Desmond Dekker, Bad Manners, King Kurt, Frenzy and The Business played at various events, including the infamous rally on the Isle of Wight in 1986. These artists increased the number of rally goers but sadly some of them were only there for the music and would not appreciate the set-up of the scooter scene. Also, among the visitors were right-wing nazi skinheads that would travel to our rallies purely to intimidate rally-goers, hurl insults around and threaten violence at the artists entertaining the scooterists. They tried this at Great Yarmouth, and we would later hear talk of the events that took place at the venue Tiffanys, where Desmond Dekker, the Jamaican ska musician, was attacked while performing. Thankfully, due to the presence and intervention of the Mansfield Monsters Scooter Club, the effect of these right-wing infiltrators was lessened, and Desmond Dekker avoided serious injury.

The following year, a group of us from Cambridge visited the Wirrina Centre in Peterborough for what we thought was a scooterist and northern soul night. Whilst racism is still very present in our society, it is not always as obvious as it was back in the 1970s and 80s, but I can understand how people that do not have white skin still, some 40 to 50 years later, walk down the street with the expectation of potential violence directed to them at any point in time. It's a crazy situation when people are still entrenched in long held views and opinions that originated in a distant and supposedly far more ignorant time in history. It soon became clear that the venue was doubling up as a meeting place for a right-wing skinhead group. Talk went round about the situation and the atmosphere was most definitely tainted with the prospect of violence. With us in our group was Chris Waldron who was black, so we were particularly on edge, and some of the people there would take unjustified offence purely by his presence. We were young, 18 to 19-years-old, and I don't remember any of us having a taste for violence. We were oblivious in all honesty to this type of situation in our normal lives and I had not personally experienced anything like this before and we were unsure of how far it may go.

Who knows what was going through Chris's mind at the time, but he was there to dance and that is what he did. Soon, his presence was noted, and he was surrounded on the dance floor by a group of right-wing thugs. Circling them were more thugs, but these ones were not looking at Chris. They were focussed on us, challenging us to intervene and help our friend. At that moment I felt useless, anything we did to help Chris would probably only increase the beating that he was to receive, as well as inflicting injuries on us. We all watched as Chris was knocked to the floor and kicked many, many times. Punches reigned down, and chairs were thrown at him as we stood there helpless in fear. Chris was taken to hospital with his injuries and the rest of us headed home. I remember being given a lift back from the venue by a mate Darren Romain, on the back of his Vespa. Leaning into the cradle backrest I was stunned and shocked by what had happened and spent the night at his parents' house before heading home in daylight. Sadly, I do not recall Chris going to another scooter rally or event after that, I may be wrong, but it would be no surprise if he hadn't.

This was not brave aggression as shown by soldiers on a battlefield defending a true and just cause but cowardly, unjust violence, it was like watching a pack of hyenas in a frenzy, having forgotten exactly what it was they were doing, lost in the kill and the bloodlust, shameful.

YOUNG, UPWARDLY MOBILE... AND STUPID

Through a friend of a friend, I was told of another scooter that was for sale. There was no information passed onto me apart from it being blue and a Lambretta, so not a lot to go on. I had a picture in my mind of a local scooter that I thought it might have been and that was quite tidy so thought I may as well have a look. A time was arranged to view the scooter and come the day I headed over to have a look. The up and over garage door housing it was lifted open to reveal a Lambretta with next to no bodywork and small petrol tank mounted in between where the riders' knees would be. I was disappointed, this was not at all the style of scooter I wanted. Really, I was after a full-bodied GP, but I thought that I may as well have a sit on the machine as I was there. Throwing my leg over the seat, sitting down, and taking hold of the handlebars made me change my mind pretty much instantly. The handlebars sat higher than on a GP, I did not feel like I was sitting on the scooter, more that I was sitting in it, and the thinly padded Snetterton race seat felt like it was positioned slightly further forward than normal.

The scooter started life as an Innocenti made Lambretta TV175 from 1963 and was originally issued with the registration number of 30 CCE. Many years later I had a photo passed on to me of it in its original full bodied and accessory adorned form, a number plate on the front mudguard confirmed its identity and the young couple sat on it were dressed very much as young smart mods of the time.

The TV175 was the Innocenti factory's first foray into a larger engine than the 125 and 150cc versions that they had used so far. It was also the first production machine in the scooter and motorcycle world to be fitted with an internal disc brake, which was seen to be more effective than the drum type brake used up to that point. Innocenti were a groundbreaking company in their time, progressing designs and technology to keep their customers invested in their product, but sadly they were unable to continue that advancement through the 1970s and ceased building the beloved Italian motor scooter. They would sell the machinery and tooling involved in the manufacturing of these machines, to companies in India who would continue to produce them for many years to come, in particular the GP model that many scooterists lusted after in the 1980s, along with other factories that were already producing them under licence around the world.

I'm sure the young mod couple sat on 30 CCE sometime in the 1960s, would have been surprised at its appearance some 20 years later. Sat on the scooter, the handlebars appeared the same, but with the addition of a yellow bodied motocross style quick action throttle and between my knees sat the petrol tank that had been poached from a NSU Quickly moped. This tank was a lovely peanut shape, wore a shiny coat of chrome plate and was mounted on an extra metal tube, leading diagonally from the steering column down to the main frame tube. Stepping off and looking at the scooter from the side, I saw a frame tube curving its way from the front wheel to the rear, where a small part of the original frame loop housed the toolbox, a petrol tank from a Lambretta LD and the thinly padded Snetterton sports seat was bolted on to the top. There were no legshields, horncasting or front mudguard, no side panels and nowhere to fit the normal rear light or number plate. And that was it, simple in its sparsity. Apart from what there was of the frame, handlebar top, engine casing and hubs, which were all coated in sky blue Hammerite paint, everything else was covered in chrome plate, a little past its best, but still shining away in the sunlight. Two small and sleek sports mudguards covered the standard size front Continental tyre and the larger sized 4.00" x 10" rear tyre which enhanced the poise of the scooter, and a number plate and small motocross style light were mounted above the rear mudguard directly behind the seat. Exiting the 225cc engine with its 34mm Amal carburettor, and working its way up passed the engine, over the kickstart and out toward the rear of the scooter was an iconic Fresco exhaust with a VW tail pipe replacing the original end can. The whole look of this scooter grabbed my attention as it would other young scooterists that saw it, and my brain was set into overdrive at how to become the owner of this machine.

Soon after I was able to persuade my bank to lend me the money needed to buy the scooter and I would hand over a significant sum of cash to the seller. Hindsight is a wonderful thing, but I would realise, where the price was concerned, that my youthfulness, naivety and enthusiasm were well and truly taken advantage of by the seller, and disappointingly in the future, my trust in him would be misplaced too. But I did now own a scooter that was unique and, as I was to find out, very well known on the rally scene and admired by scooter and motorcycle riders alike. The scooter was later taken home and parked up as I needed to pass my full motorcycle test to ride it legally. I would own the scooter for 21 years rebuilding it a couple of times, making it my own, and it would often be recognised while out riding from its earlier sky-blue incarnation.

I couldn't resist the temptation riding it though, and with some strategically placed 125cc stickers and a couple of L-Plates, its true guise was hidden from the unknowing which, along with a little white lie told to the relevant authorities, made it appear that I was riding a learner legal scooter.

Anyone that had the slightest idea about scooters and engines would question a 125cc machine fitted with a huge 34mm Amal carburettor. This was quite common practice back then, and still happens today, but I was a young lad not fully realising the consequences of being caught out. A year later I would take and pass my full motorcycle test the day before my provisional licence ran out, thankfully ending the need for L-Plates for ever, but not before cadging an illicit lift on Dwain's scooter. We were both in town, him on his 50 Special and me having caught the bus. The offer of a lift home using a spare crash helmet he had with him was too tempting, so removing the conveniently magnetic L-Plates, I jumped on the back and off we went. Riding along, Dwain spotted a police car as we went through a junction and decided to quickly take a left turn off the main road. Now of course, that action by a couple of young herberts on a small scooter that you would imagine would need L-Plates, is a red rag to any self-respecting police officer, and so this one quickly followed and pulled us over. It was a fair cop though, and I found myself walking home anyway. We were both duly reported for the traffic offence, pleading guilty by post, and received fines and penalty points on our licences. This endorsement on my licence and one that I was soon to pick up at the forthcoming Isle of Wight scooter rally have been the only ones picked up in my time of riding but, in all honesty, that is only down to adopting the respectful "yes officer, no officer" approach on more than one occasion or just not getting caught. These days, a vastly reduced police force with far more important things to do and with me looking more responsible, being pulled over is a far less common occurrence and I have not had a tug from the law in a long, long time.

LIFE'S A RIOT

At 6 o'clock on the Friday night leading into the August Bank Holiday weekend, a small group of us head off on our scooters to the Isle of Wight scooter rally of 1986. Only 15 miles from Cambridge we stopped for a break in the marketplace car park of a local town. I can only imagine stopping so soon was down to raging testosterone and someone in the group wanting to eye up the local girls making their way out for a night on the town. After a while, we all got ready to set off again after having comprehensively failed at convincing any of the local girls that we were worthy of their attention (no surprise there), but my cutdown decided to be uncooperative and refused to start. Eventually, and probably more by luck than judgement, we got the engine running again despite my best attempt to end the weekend early when, as I was running along and trying to bump start the scooter, I looked up to see myself heading straight for a parked car at the very moment as the engine fired into life. A quick and instinctive pull on the handlebars took me safely clear of the car with the others watching in horror. Not long after that, heading south on the old A10, the VW tailpipe on my exhaust decided to make a break for freedom, shooting itself out of its securing clamp never to be seen again. We turned back and tried to find it but with no luck. After a while I was banished to the back of the group as my scooter was now so loud no one could bear to ride behind me for fear of permanent hearing damage. When we finally reach the island the next day, a police officer in Newport with sensitive hearing was not happy with the din my exhaust made so issued me with a ticket that would become the second endorsement on my driving licence.

How long we expected the journey to take I don't know, but with the unscheduled stops and breaks for cigarettes and food, we weren't making fast progress. None of us having full motorcycle licences yet meant we had to ride through London rather than around it on the M25. It must have been well past midnight when we decided to stop at a closed petrol station somewhere in South West London to see if we could get a bit of sleep around the back in the shelter of some business units. We unrolled our sleeping bags (we still did not take tents with us to a rally yet) and tried to settle down. This didn't last long though; someone had gone for a wander and discovered a jumble of prosthetic limbs and mannequins in a window of one of the business units. At that time of night, the whole situation was quite surreal and just a little bit eery, so in a fit of giggles, they just had to share what they had found with everyone else. There was no chance of getting any sleep now, so after a while we packed our kit away and got back on the road and headed for Portsmouth.

The ride down to the Isle of Wight along the old A3, was always memorable, through the Devils Punchbowl, Liphook, Petersfield and past Butser Hill,

Leaving my lock at the Portsmouth ferry terminal

and was probably where I began to really appreciate the ride to a scooter rally, avoiding motorways where possible and taking the time to enjoy the roads and scenery. Arriving in Portsmouth around six or seven o'clock in the morning, the lack of sleep was not a major problem due to our youth and the adrenaline running through our veins. But before we could board the ferry, the local police were making all the scooterists leave any tools and chains behind, that could potentially be used as a weapon and then claimed back on the way home.

Having to take a ferry to this rally gave it a special atmosphere that no other scooter rally had and thinking back nearly 40 years ago while writing this, I drag out some old photographs to refresh my memory of the weekend. My favourite picture is one of us all on the Portsmouth to Ryde ferry, on the first crossing of the day. When we boarded the ferry, word went round that as we were "at sea" the bar was open and so, at eight o'clock in the morning, we all shot up the stairs to the bar and grabbed a couple of beers each.

Early morning beers on the Isle of Wight ferry

The photo was taken for me by Carl Cartwright, he is the only one of us not in the shot and his beer is on the roof of a car. We are all gurning away back at him, some of us are holding a drink or puffing on a fag. Steve Brown looks quite tame at that moment despite his freshly cropped hair which gives him a menacing skinhead look, Tom Quigley is giving a thumbs up and is dwarfed by a skinny Chris Manning who wears a big cheesy grin, then there's me with my flat top, squashed by my crash helmet, beer in hand and a fag sticking out of my mouth, Mark "Billy" Bridgeman is playing the clown with an empty plastic pint glass turned upside down on his head and Chris "Crazy" O'Connor stands slightly to the side quietly, puffing on a cigarette.

After hitting the bar, we mingled with bemused holiday makers before heading back to our scooters, starting them up far too early and then sitting there blipping the throttle creating a smog of fumes. This was a massive buzz and being amongst such a mass of scooters and riding down the ramp and onto the island to spend a weekend away from normality, is still seared in my memory even now.

We headed to the campsite where we met up with other friends that had travelled down from Cambridge, friends that a year earlier I hadn't yet met but now regularly shared a beer with, met up with at a gig or, as now, travelled to a scooter rally with. Once on the island, we really felt we had achieved something just by arriving. The atmosphere on site was calm and relaxed and another picture shows our group sat in a field with a few scooters scattered around them; Crazy's TV200 partially obscured by a standing Billy, Steves P-Range next to Chris' sky blue and white GP and just in the picture, the tiny seat of Toms yellow street racer Little Lamb Bee. They would have been chatting about the ride down, wondering what the weekend had in store, or just chilling after the journey down, good times.

Ever since then, the real draw for me, one that the Isle of Wight has over any other scooter rally in the UK, is that the weekend isn't confined to just one town. Riding around the island we would always see other scooterists doing exactly the same thing as us, exploring, taking in the scenery and maybe stopping on a seafront somewhere for an ice cream or a crafty ride on one of the 20p kids arcade rides that was always a special treat when you were little, I know we did.

Early morning at the campsite on the Isle of Wight

ISLE OF WIGHT
POCKET MAP

Based upon the Ordnance Survey map with the permission of the Controller of H.M.S.O. Crown copyright reserved.
• Aubrey Carne, Seaview, Isle of Wight, 1988

INDEX

G3	Adgestone	F3	Downend	C4	Mottistone	H3	St. Helens
B3	Afton	F3	Downs, The	A4	Needles, The	H3	St. Lawrence
A3	Alum Bay	G8	Durnoss	E5	Nettlecombe	F5	Sandford
G3	Alverstone	D1	East Cowes	H2	Nettlestone	F4	Sandown
G2	Apsey	E1	Egypt Point	E3	Newbridge	G4	Sandown Bay
F4	Apse Heath	G2	Elmfield	F3	Newchurch	G2	Sandy Way
F3	Arreton	F2	Fishbourne	C2	Newtown	H2	Seaview
G2	Ashey	H3	Foreland	C3	Ningwood	C3	Shalcombe
D4	Atherfield Green	E3	Forest Side	E3	Nilton	C3	Shalfleet
D3	Barton	B3	Freshwater	H3	No Man's Land Fort	G4	Shanklin
H3	Bembridge	B3	Freshwater Bay	H2	Northwood	F5	Shide
H3	Bembridge Airport	C2	Gatcombe	B3	Norton	D4	Shorwell
H3	Bembridge Harbour	F4	Godshill	B3	Norton Green	E5	Southford
B5	Binstey	G1	Gosport	G2	Oakfield	H1	Southsea
G2	Binstead	E3	Gurville	G4	Old Village	H1	Spit Bank Fort
G2	Blackwater	D1	Gurnard	F1	Osborne Bay	F5	Spithead
F5	Bonchurch	C2	Hamstead	E2	Parkhurst	F4	Spring Vale
B3	Bouldnor	F2	Havenstreet	D2	Parkhurst Forest	E1	Springhill
D4	Bowcombe	G2	Haylands	G2	Ponchard	E3	Staplers
B3	Brading	N	Horse Sand Fort	D2	Porchfield	F5	Steephill
D4	Branstone	C4	Hulverstone	H1	Portsmouth	B3	Thorley
D4	Brighstone	E3	Hunny Hill	H2	Priory Bay	B3	Thorley Street
C4	Brighstone Forest	A3	Hurst Castle	H2	Puckpool Point	D2	Thorness Bay
C4	Brighstone Bay	E6	Kingates	D5	Pyle	A3	Totland
G3	Brook	E4	Kingston	D2	Rew Street	A3	Totland Bay
C3	Calbourne	F2	Kite Hill	D2	River Medina	F5	Undercliff, The
B5	Carisbrooke	G4	Lake	B3	River Yar	F4	Upper Hyde
F5	Chale	H3	Lane End	E4	River Yar	G2	Upton
D5	Chale Bay	D4	Little Atherfield	E4	Rookley	F5	Ventnor
D5	Chale Green	B2	Littletown	E4	Roud	C3	Wellow
E3	Chillerton	F2	Lowtherville	E4	Ryde	H3	Whippingham
E3	Clatterford	G5	Luccombe Village	F5	St. Boniface Down	H3	Whitecliff Bay
A3	Colwell Bay	A1	Lymington	E5	St. Catherine's Pt.	F4	Whiteley Bank
B4	Compton Bay	F4	Mark's Corner	A3	Todand	E3	Whitwell
E5	Compton Down	E3	Merstone	D2	Thorness Bay	F4	Winford
E1	Cowes	A3	Middleton	A3	Todand Bay	F2	Woodside
C2	Cranmore	C4	Moortown			F2	Wootton
H3	Culver Cliff					E2	Wootton Bridge
						F2	Wootton Common
						F5	Wroxall
						D4	Yafford
						B3	Yarmouth
						G3	Yaverland

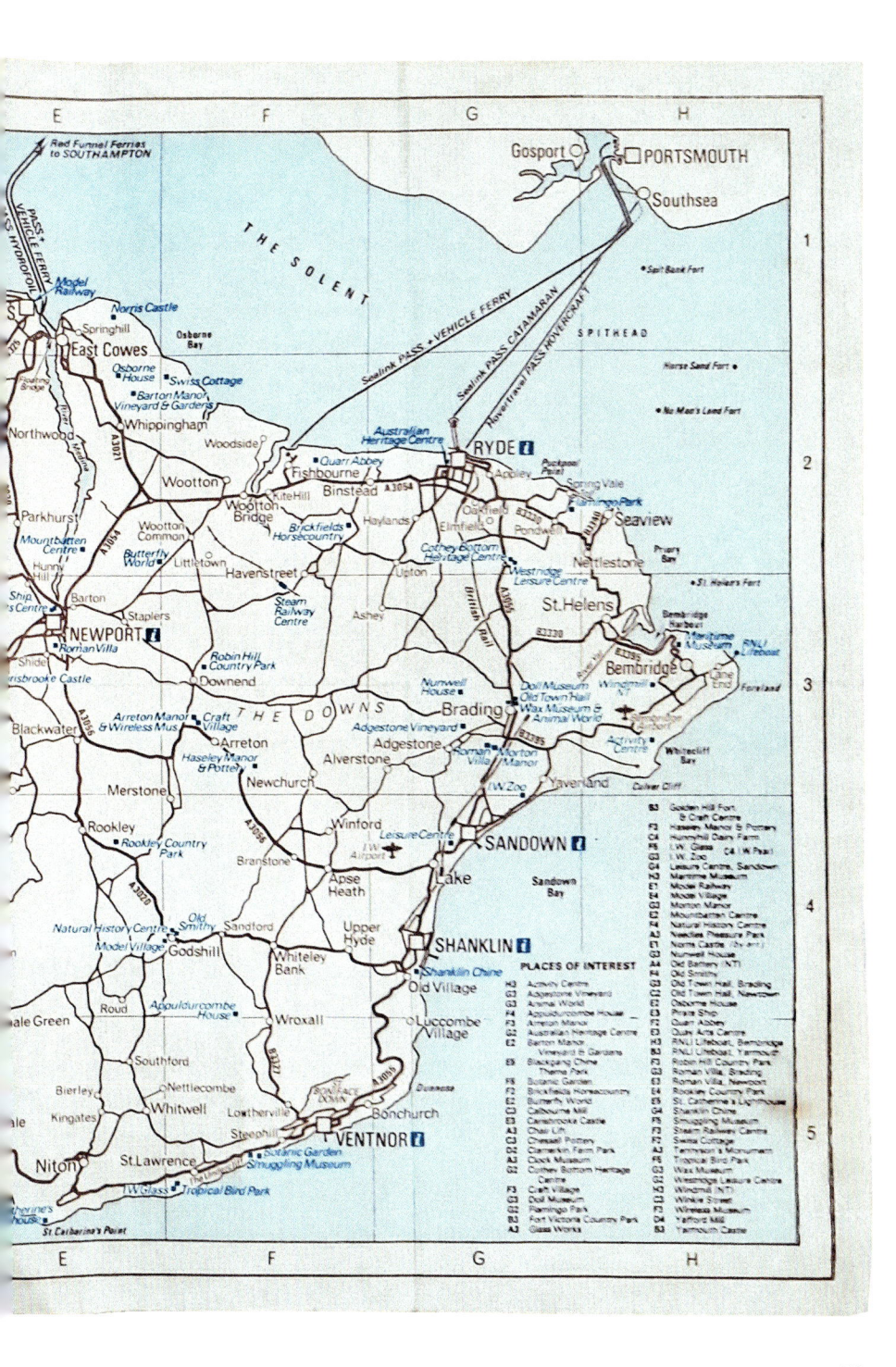

Map of the Isle of Wight

Places shown on map:

- Red Funnel Ferries to SOUTHAMPTON
- PASS+ VEHICLE FERRY / PASS HYDROFOIL
- Model Railway
- Springhill
- East Cowes
- Norris Castle
- Osborne Bay
- Osborne House
- Swiss Cottage
- Barton Manor Vineyard & Gardens
- Northwood
- Whippingham
- Woodside
- Fishbourne
- Quarr Abbey
- Binstead
- Kite Hill
- Wootton Bridge
- Wootton
- Wootton Common
- Brickfields Horsecountry
- Haylands
- Appley
- RYDE
- Puckpool Point
- Spring Vale
- Flamingo Park
- Seaview
- Oakfield
- Elmfield
- Pondwell
- Nettlestone
- Priory Bay
- Parkhurst
- Mountbatten Centre
- Butterfly World
- Littletown
- Havenstreet
- Upton
- Cotney Bottom Heritage Centre
- Westridge Leisure Centre
- St. Helens
- St. Helen's Fort
- Bembridge Harbour
- Maritime Museum
- RNLI Lifeboat
- Hunny Hill
- Barton
- Ship's Centre
- Staplers
- NEWPORT
- Roman Villa
- Shide
- Carisbrooke Castle
- Steam Railway Centre
- Ashey
- Bembridge
- Windmill (NT)
- Bine End
- Foreland
- Blackwater
- Arreton Manor & Wireless Mus.
- Craft Village
- Haseley Manor & Pottery
- Arreton
- THE DOWNS
- Downend
- Nunwell House
- Brading
- Doll Museum
- Old Town Hall
- Wax Museum & Animal World
- Adgestone Vineyard
- Adgestone
- Roman Villa
- Morton Manor
- Activity Centre
- Whitecliff Bay
- Merstone
- Newchurch
- Alverstone
- I.W. Zoo
- Yaverland
- Culver Cliff
- Rookley
- Rookley Country Park
- Winford
- Leisure Centre
- I.W. Airport
- Branstone
- SANDOWN
- Sandown Bay
- Apse Heath
- Lake
- Natural History Centre
- Old Smithy
- Sandford
- Upper Hyde
- SHANKLIN
- Model Village
- Godshill
- Whiteley Bank
- Shanklin Chine
- Old Village
- Appuldurcombe House
- Roud
- Wroxall
- Luccombe Village
- Vale Green
- Southford
- Bierley
- Nettlecombe
- Dunnose
- Kingates
- Whitwell
- Lowtherville
- Bonchurch
- Steephill
- VENTNOR
- Niton
- St. Lawrence
- Botanic Garden / Smuggling Museum
- I.W.Glass
- Tropical Bird Park
- St. Catherine's Point
- St. Catherine's Lighthouse
- Gosport
- PORTSMOUTH
- Southsea
- THE SOLENT
- Sealink PASS+ VEHICLE FERRY
- Hovertravel PASS ROVERCRAFT
- Sealink PASS CATAMARAN
- SPITHEAD
- Spit Bank Fort
- Horse Sand Fort
- No Man's Land Fort
- Australian Heritage Centre

PLACES OF INTEREST

H3	Activity Centre
G3	Adgestone Vineyard
F4	Animal World
G2	Appuldurcombe House
G3	Arreton Manor
G2	Australian Heritage Centre
E3	Barton Manor Vineyard & Gardens
E5	Blackgang Chine Theme Park
F5	Botanic Garden
F2	Brickfields Horsecountry
F2	Butterfly World
C3	Calbourne Mill
E3	Carisbrooke Castle
C3	Chair Lift
F5	Chessell Pottery
A3	Clock Museum
G2	Cotney Bottom Heritage Centre
F3	Craft Village
G3	Doll Museum
F5	Flamingo Park
B3	Fort Victoria Country Park
A3	Glass Works
B3	Golden Hill Fort & Craft Centre
G3	Haseley Manor & Pottery
C4	Hunnyhill Dairy Farm
F5	I.W. Glass
G4	I.W. Zoo
G4	Leisure Centre, Sandown
H3	Maritime Museum
E1	Model Railway
E4	Model Village
G3	Morton Manor
E2	Mountbatten Centre
E4	Natural History Centre
F2	Nettlestone
G3	Nunwell House
E1	Norris Castle (by am)
E4	Old Battery (NT)
E4	Old Smithy
G3	Old Town Hall, Brading
C2	Old Town Hall, Newtown
E3	Osborne House
F2	Priory Bay
E3	Quarr Abbey
H3	RNLI Lifeboat, Bembridge
F3	RNLI Lifeboat, Yarmouth
F3	Robin Hill Country Park
G3	Roman Villa, Brading
E3	Roman Villa, Newport
F3	Rookley Country Park
E5	St. Catherine's Lighthouse
G4	Shanklin Chine
F5	Smuggling Museum
E2	Steam Railway Centre
F2	Swiss Cottage
A1	Tennyson's Monument
F5	Tropical Bird Park
F4	Wax Museum
G2	Westridge Leisure Centre
D3	Windmill (NT)
C3	Winkle Street
E5	Wireless Museum
D4	Yafford Mill
B3	Yarmouth Castle

Just a big kid!   Blackgang Chine on the Isle of Wight

At Ventnor there was a large 3D concrete map of the island, and I am sure we weren't the only rally goers that would clamber across for a photo opportunity and which I was pleased to see was still there when I returned there years later on a family holiday, repeating the moment with my kids. Riding around the island we visited Sandown, Shanklin, Ventnor and Blackgang Chine, where we would climb onto the now redundant old military vehicles and stand next to the fibreglass dinosaurs in the theme park for photos, before getting that ticket for my loud exhaust in Newport, and then being turned away by a police roadblock when we found ourselves too close to Parkhurst prison.

It would be a while before the main aim of a rally weekend was hitting the pub as soon as we arrived and of course this was still well before all day opening in the UK, but we did of course have a few pints in the evening, it would be rude not to. The pub's regulars were very welcoming and probably thought we were all mad, looking how we did and traipsing all that way on our little scooters. After the pub, our thoughts turned to where we were going to spend the night. Looking back now, I am amazed how we used to wing it with our lack of plans, taking only a sleeping bag for accommodation. Did I take a toothbrush and a nice little co-ordinated wash bag and towel with a range of shower gels? Well, if I did, I have truly erased it from my memory, so it's safe to assume that we all took on the role of Stig of the Dump for the duration of the rally. The following year would be when I started actually taking a tent before progressing onto splashing out on a room in a bed and breakfast hotel, but for the moment a spacious, old-fashioned bus shelter that we had found, with wooden slatted benches and plenty of room for us and our scooters, would do the job for one night.

Luckily for us, we didn't attract any attention from the police, and I had a very satisfying sleep wrapped up in my ex-army sleeping bag. The town council's bin men didn't have much consideration for us though, giving us an early morning wakeup call with the clanging of bin lids as the black bags were removed and thrown onto the dustcart. Shortly after that, sensing that we were being watched after hearing footsteps stop in front of the bus shelter, I peered out from my sleeping bag and could see two scootergirls taking photos of us all cosily wrapped up and seemingly asleep. At the same time someone else noticed we were being watched and stirred. This movement then caused us all to rouse from our sleep and soon we were all chatting with the two girls. They returned shortly afterwards with several bags of crisps to be shared between us. After chatting for a bit, the girls said goodbye then a while later we decided to head for breakfast and a cuppa at a seaside café across the road, only to find the two girls there enjoying their own breakfast so, as we were such polite lads, we joined them and chatted some more, poor girls.

You are here! Ventnor on the Isle of Wight. L to R Me, Carl Ireland, Steve Brown and Chris Manning

Heading home

Being watched, in the bus shelter

Probably brought on by the thought of another 12-hour return journey we all decided to head home to Cambridge on the Sunday, fitting in a stopover in Lewisham, South East London. Chris told us that we could stop over at a squat his sister was living in, so we headed in that direction. I don't know if he had prepped her in advance, but she took the arrival of our scruffy and probably smelly presence in her stride and that was where we spent the night, crashed out on the floor of a big old Victorian house. Just a few years later, I would find myself regularly in the same area having met a girl through scooter friends Jackie Wilson and her boyfriend David Childs. Lesley, the girl, was shown a photo of me and told "You'll like him," but seeing a shaven headed scooter boy, I don't think she was so sure to start with. Soon afterwards I would meet her in our local pub one Friday night when Jackie, her sister, dragged her out for the night. In my increasingly drunken state that night I must have made an impression. We bumped into each other again when she was dragged out the following night to see a mod band, The Moment, for a gig at the infamous Cambridge venue The Sea Cadet Hall. A while later we started going out together, and after 6 months of racking up hundreds of miles travelling backwards and forwards along the M11 visiting her, I would move down to live with her in Catford. She would spend many miles as my pillion, get her own scooter and go on to pass her motorcycle test. While we lived in the area, I would regularly visit Kickstart Motorcycles for scooter parts and entertainment from Simon behind the counter, before moving to nearby Plumstead Common and then returning to Cambridge having started a family.

We left the squat and rode home the next day. Taking a wrong turn, we ended up on the M11. "Sod it! We're here now we may as well carry on" was the general consensus, so removing our L-Plates and because the traditional Bank Holiday weather had finally arrived and it was raining, we continued along the motorway as far as Cambridge, carried along by the thought of a hot bath, fresh clothes, and endless cups of tea on arrival. Whether it was when we arrived home or during the previous night's stop I can't remember now, but we soon heard of the infamous riot that had taken place at the rally campsite. A mix of exorbitant beer prices and rally goers that were not there for the scooters, but for the Oi based bands that were playing there that night, caused the trouble that took place. I'm quite happy we left when we did. To have witnessed such chaos; the beer tent being burnt to the ground, the scooter dealers ransacked for their stock and vehicles being overturned or torched, would have had a negative effect on anyone wanting to attend further events. I imagine the mood the following morning amongst the majority of scooterists still on the island, would have been pensive with a lot of time spent discussing the previous night's destruction as well as the future of the scooter scene.

L to R Chris O'Connor, Carl Cartwright and me

Thankfully, the people that made up the National Runs Committee (NRC) that organised the rallies were part of the scooter scene too, enjoying the rallies themselves, and they were not prepared to allow the riot to end such a great phenomenon. They would find themselves spending untold hours liaising with local councils and the police, who would continually put barriers up to our presence in "their" towns and resorts. Membership to the NRC became a necessity, ID cards were introduced along with a level of secrecy regarding times and places of scooter rallies that hadn't been seen before. The following year, our presence was under microscopic scrutiny in every town that we visited. Bands were not to be found playing at a rally until some years later. This was purposefully done to reduce non-scootering incomers and because venues were often not prepared for their premises to be hired to the organisers in fear of a repeat of the riot that had caused all these restrictions. I do know that I was, and I'm sure many others were and still are, extremely grateful to the people involved in the NRC that were motivated enough to put their time and effort into ensuring the continuation of our scooter rallies, following the events of that Sunday night in August 1986.

Around that time, frequent industrial disruptions around the country with steel works being shut down, the motor industry being run into the ground and workers striking were regularly mentioned on the Six O'clock News, along with the ever-increasing number of unemployed. The most infamous of these was the Miner's Strike around 1985, with violent clashes between strikers and the police under the control of Maggie Thatcher and her Conservative government. Even now, nearly 40 years later, it is not unusual for the subject to come up in conversation at a rally with a northern scooterist, who will tell you of the devastating effect that shutting down the mines had on the surrounding communities. The long running dispute would give the police some preparation time for the scooter rallies of the next few years, following the now infamous Isle of Wight National scooter rally. Extra police would be drafted in on several occasions to watch our behaviour in the seaside towns we visited. Roadblocks on the outskirts of towns were used for the first time to search riders, inspect scooters, and to rifle through toolboxes looking for offensive weapons and drugs, before they were allowed to continue on to the rally.

But despite everything negative that happened that weekend on the Isle of Wight, it remains my favourite scooter run of all the national rallies that I attended, the island is a special place to hold a scooter rally, even now in the 21st century. The rally was moved to different dates in following years because of the fallout from the riot, but for many years now it has found itself a regular occurrence every August bank holiday. A lot of time has passed and a scooter rally in town is no longer seen as a threat by the authorities while local businesses, shop keepers, publicans and hoteliers are all very happy to receive the extra income that scooterists bring into their town.

The Isle of Wight is a variation of what it was back then, but it is still a scooter rally. Different people want different things from the event. There will be people still attending the Isle of Wight rally that would have been present on that fateful night as well as a huge number of newcomers to the scene. While some people transport their scooters to the island in a van for maybe their only rally of the year or strut around the island putting on a display worthy of any peacock, some old hands (but not all) will look on in consternation at the people that attend the modern-day rally, maybe because of how they dress, what scooters they ride or whether they actually ride their scooters there or not. But there are no rules, and nobody is forced to attend. There will be a club somewhere around the country putting on a small rally or a scooter related event most weekends if the Isle of Wight is not to your taste. The shops and businesses welcome the rally goers, and the money they bring in with open arms, and the rally is still an impressive event, just a bit different to the one of years before. I went back to the island for the rally three or four times between 2004 and 2012. While it had changed a lot, I still enjoyed myself with the mates I was with, rallies are always what you make them, but I generally attend smaller events now, probably with a daytime riding element, and a chance to have a few beers and a chat in the evening. People have mellowed with age and that can bring a different feel to a rally compared to those of years ago. They still want to enjoy riding their scooters but maybe in a different way to how they did when they were 18, when they were happy to be one of the great unwashed for a weekend, drunk and sitting in a field with little in the way of facilities.

Viv McCann messing around

SMALL TOWN ENGLAND

At the start of 1987 I had a handful of National Rallies under my belt. The scooter community in Cambridge was building. I found people that were in the years below me at school were now getting into the scooter scene and I met more people through friends of friends, at gigs and not forgetting the Saturday afternoon meet-up in town. As a younger teenager, wandering around Cambridge town centre could be a fraught time and I was always aware of the danger of catching the eye of a local thug looking to make a name for themselves as a "hard case". The 1980s were an oppressive and violent time. We didn't have to worry about weapons being used against us in the way that knife crime has become so prevalent in recent years, but youth culture was tribal and being in the wrong tribe at the wrong time could lead to a good kicking. Back then, it was much more obvious which strain of youth movement people belonged to, so pickings could be easy and there were often clashes between punks, teds, or skinheads. But, wandering around the local town centre in amongst a group of scooterists, I found that people didn't try to intimidate us but that we might actually be the unwitting intimidators with our appearance, like one lad who had a full on mohican haircut, wore a studded leather jacket, big boots and would carry his pet rat Boris around with him.

Viv had been given the name by schoolmates, because of his resemblance to Vyvyan the spiky ginger haired psychopathic student from the telly series The Young Ones, and with his old school Mohican haircut, he made quite a picture. All these years later he's still known to everyone as Viv, except his mum and dad who call him his proper name Michael (McCann). But these days he would now struggle to grow a mohican of that size and colour due to the onset of middle age. Our crowd were a mixed bunch from different tribes; scooterists, mods, punks, skinheads and psychobillies. Despite looking like a right bunch of misfits that should have been fighting each other, we were all out just to have a good time. On Saturday lunchtimes we would meet at The Ancient Druids pub for a few drinks, all with the common connection of scooters and the scooter scene, to talk rubbish or to make plans for the next rally, and with this ever-increasing circle of scooter mates, I would travel around the country, sometimes under my own steam and sometimes cadging a lift if my scooter was off the road, to attend scooter rallies, custom shows or club events. Simple and fun times.

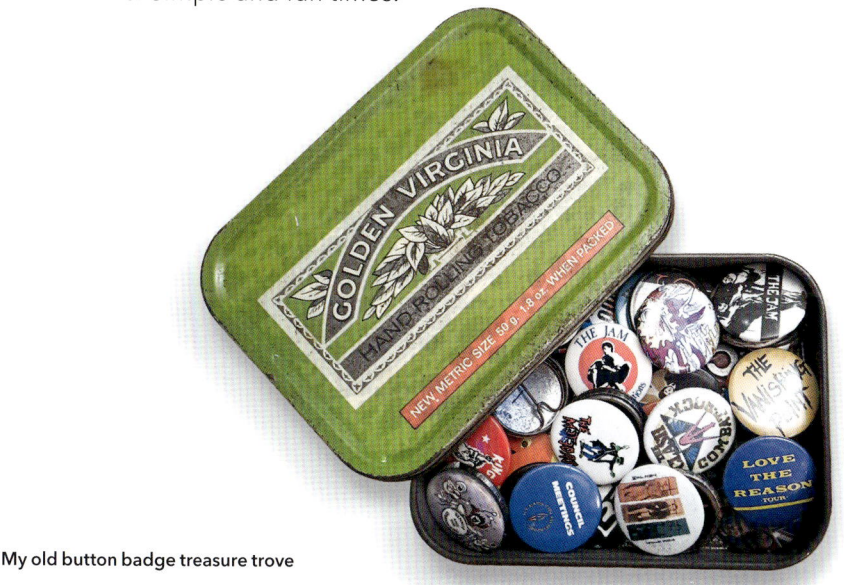

My old button badge treasure trove

IF YOU AIN'T GOT A TICKET YOU CAN'T COME IN

In the 1950s there were many scooter clubs with large memberships attending rallies, gymkhanas, and sporting events. These rallies were not beer fuelled gatherings attended by hordes of unruly scooterists as in the 1980s, but much more organised and sedate. I'm sure they enjoyed a glass or two of real ale in a dimpled pint pot but maybe not to the point of drinking a pub dry, which was not uncommon on a national rally, and rather than a MA1 flight jacket you were more likely to see them wearing a substantial duffle coat and woolly hat. Club recognition was particularly important, with members maybe wearing matching overalls or flying club pennants from their scooters while riding them in formation as part of a display. The sporting side of scooter riding would include reliability trials promoting the different marques or events like the Scottish Six Day Trials, the Isle of Man Scooter week in the early 1960s or eventually, in the early 1970s, short circuit scooter racing.

There are always people that want to ride their scooters harder, faster or for longer. Racing, along with sprinting, are two ways that can be achieved. Since those pioneering days, scooter racing hasn't really gone away and there are riders such as the Legendary Arthur Francis, Ray Kemp of AF Rayspeed, Ron Moss of Supertune, Norrie Kerr and Dave Webster of Midland Scooter Centre, Bob West and the Frankland brothers of Taffspeed Racing among others, whose names were spoken of in awe and are still revered to this day, as well as the scooterists of the 1980s that took up and continued the racing mantle, people like Jem Booth, Stuart Day and Paul Green. Luckily scooter racing has been going through a resurgence for some time now. The standard of riding and the leaps and bounds in knowledge and technology has really developed the sport with more people getting involved and becoming bona fide club racers. Scooter sprinting too has been active recently. Since the time when people like Fred Willingham, Frank Osgerby and Richard Baker with his scooter Frightened Chicken used to tear up the strip in the search for more speed and faster times. Sprinting has continued to hold an interest in people looking to achieve the fastest possible straight-line speed from a humble Lambretta or Vespa. It is astounding really that sprint speeds approaching 120mph are not uncommon while recently riders such as Eric Cope and Adie Horrocks have gone past 120mph and Keith Terry reached a recorded 132mph to set a FIM World Speed Record on a full bodied Lambretta in 2020. To the average road rider, the speeds achieved, either in a straight line or around a race track, are something that can only be dreamed of, but where we do benefit is from the technology used in these settings being passed on to the road rider in the form of new engine kits or parts designed to make our machines faster or more reliable, or if we are really lucky, both!

In the boom of the late 1970s and the 1980s, scooter clubs were formed but more along the lines of the northern scooter clubs that thrived in the 1970s than the sporting clubs of the 50s and 60s. The newer clubs were more likely to be a group of mates customising their scooters, making them go faster and drinking together or posing around town on their machines vying for the attention of the opposite sex, but more often gaining the attention of the "old bill" and the might of the law. They would travel en-mass to a seaside town for local weekend rallies, which were inherited from the mods of the 1960s and their outings to places like Hastings, Margate, and Clacton over bank holiday weekends. Rallies in the 1970s were mainly northern based and informally set up, maybe with clubs from nearby towns spreading details by word of mouth, until Martin Dixon's early scooter magazine Northern Mod Scene (which later became Scootermania) would share the information. Scooter clubs of the 1980s varied in size, from a handful of mates to dozens of riders, and if they were affiliated, they could send a representative, known as a Number 1, to a yearly meeting to decide on when and where the following year's rallies would be held. They would identify themselves with club names that could be wacky (Colchester Scooter Willies SC), self-explanatory (Alcoholic Rats SC) or just plainly ridiculous (Maggie Thatcher's Left Tit SC), no one can say that scooterists in the 1980s did not have a sense of humour, or more traditionally with names like Great Yarmouth Wasps SC or Radstock Devils SC.

In Cambridge, the Desert Rats SC and Just Another SC were the two main clubs in the second half of the 1980s, and they would regularly get together, whether in town for a few drinks or on a rally somewhere around the country. I've always preferred not being aligned to a club really. This meant that there were no allegiances to follow, so who you met up for a few beers or who you rode to a rally with was not a problem and of course there were no club rules to stick to or subs to pay, but after riding to a few rallies and often being given a lift when I was scooterless by Jonny (Roy) Hunter of the Desert Rats, I joined them for a while.

The Desert Rats were a good crowd of rally-goers who made The Rose & Crown pub near the centre of Cambridge their local and were welcomed despite monopolising the pool table in the public bar. Tom Rix was Number 1 and best mate Jonny was his partner in crime if there was any piss-taking to be had.

The rest of the club were made up by Darren and Alison Romain, David Childs and Jackie Wilson, Mark "Billy" Bridgeman, Mark "Bubbles" Nunn, Sally "Bev" Bevan, Jon Diver, Brian Gourley, John Edge, Craig Northfield and Phillip Parker. There will have been a few others and apologies if I haven't remembered you here. Apart from the drinking, dancing and rallies, there was the club do where you could again drink and dance the night away but closer to home with many other scooterists from around the area, while raising money for the local charity MAGPAS who provided emergency medical care for people involved in road traffic collisions and still operate today, and so was particularly appropriate to us.

Desert Rats SC on the way to Great Yarmouth

Desert Rats Christmas Do 1987

Desert Rats SC Charity donation to MAGPAS

One year, Viv demonstrated how not to ride a scooter. Having had a good night at the Desert Rats do, he started to make his way home in a state that was slightly the worse for alcoholic consumption. Just outside the hall he bumped into a group of friends, one of which had arrived on his tuned Vespa small frame. Somehow, despite being as drunk as a skunk, Viv persuaded the owner to "giz us a go." Handing over his pride and joy the owner watched as Viv started the engine, sat astride the machine, and promptly lost all ability to function and control the scooter. The clutch was engaged, and first gear selected as he grabbed a handful of throttle. The revs soared skywards and at the same time he quickly let go of the clutch. In a flurry of smoke and noise the scooter fishtailed at speed across the car park trying to send its rider into orbit, he clung on for a few moments before having no choice but to release his grip and flounder on the tarmac. The scooter then careered off before coming to a scraping halt some way off. Viv stumbled to his feet and looked on agog, trying to work out what had just happened while the owner just crumbled in a quivering wreck wondering how to rewind time.

Desert Rats Sc and Just Another SC, Morecambe 1988

Just Another SC were made up of quite a few people that were mostly two or three years younger and that I knew from school. Not too far from Cambridge, were the Huntingdon Ratshaggers SC and from Newmarket, The Paralytics SC, and The Rat & Rodent SC. The rat theme in club names was popular all over the country, stemming from the pyschobilly band King Kurt who used a rat caricature in their record sleeve artwork and T-shirts. The Ratshaggers were a mix of scooter skinheads and psychobilly types while The Rat & Rodent SC were skinheads with a reputation of right-wing political views. There was some friction between them and non-right-wing scooter clubs because of their differing views and considering the problems on scooter rallies around the time this is not surprising. Despite their skewed political beliefs, they were all scooter riders and could name the well-respected scooters Alien and England Expects, as belonging to their members. The Paralytics were quite different, it is easy to see where their priorities lay from their club's name, and they too had some nice scooters in their club, one of which was a well-known and influential Vespa, The Wall.

Anyone with a good understanding of the skinhead culture knows that it is not a straightforward one. According to the newspapers, all were violent football hooligans and racist thugs. No one can deny that being an element in the history of the skinhead movement, but being or looking like a skinhead did not mean that was the principle being followed. The look was a continuation of mod, tough looking but smart and well-presented. Ben Sherman, Levi, Fred Perry and Dr Martens were popular brands of clothing worn to achieve the required look and in the late 1980s, many scooter riders found themselves revisiting the style, including me, but there was also the later 1970s style of skinhead that maybe preferred the Oi music of bands like The 4-Skins, Cockney Rejects, Skrewdriver and Cocksparrer. There were lots of contradictions in the movement with many skinheads enjoying and dancing to Jamaican ska or soul music played by musicians of Afro-Caribbean origin and the new culturally inclusive bands on the 2 Tone record label, yet at the same time, some of them would perpetrate harassment and violence towards that very same group of people for no other reason than the colour of their skin. There was a definite change of atmosphere on scooter rallies around this time because of the non-scooter people and their dodgy political ideology, but thankfully there are plenty of others that didn't share this view. There was a big push to "Keep Politics Out of Scootering" as well as the beginnings of the left-wing skinhead movement SHARP (Skinheads Against Racial Prejudice) to balance the scales in the favour of scooter riders wanting to enjoy the rallies in safety and who didn't judge someone purely on the colour of their skin or where they came from.

NRC membership card

Desert Rats SC DIY magazines

THERE AND BACK AGAIN, TO SEE HOW FAR IT IS

1987 was the first year where rally details were not freely available (following the Isle of Wight riot) and once the venues were finalised, the National Runs Committee (NRC) would release information to affiliated clubs and solo riders by a postal newsletter. This seemed a bit draconian at the time and could have been seen as contrary to the independence and freedom that the rallies gave to us, but without the ID cards, the secrecy and the hours of negotiations with the police and local authorities by the NRC, then scooter rallies would not have continued in the same form or scale that they had reached at that point. On the plus side, everyone from that time that did join the NRC must have a small collection of ID cards with dodgy looking pictures of themselves taken in the old pull the curtain across style photobooths. Photographic evidence to show their kids and grandchildren of the wacky haircuts and gurning features from way back when.

The year was a busy one, with a good mix of rallies, custom shows, and trips to venues such as The Pink Toothbrush in Rayleigh, Essex, to see bands like Bad Manners, King Kurt, and the Meteors. I have memories of minibus trips to The Pink Toothbrush, with its sticky carpets and who knows what else trodden into it, with Cambridge mates (it's strange what our memories store, if we remember accurately that is?), and a hire-coach trip to see Cambridge band The Men from Uncle in Colchester, with mod and scooterist Andy Lindsay on guitar, supporting the Guana Batz.

Before the previous year's riot there had been bands playing at DISC 85 (its full title being "Donnington International Scooter Classic", which was far more glamorous than the reality) and several bands played at the Doncaster version of DISC rally in 1986 on a stage in front of the racecourse grandstand. Sat on the grass in sunny Doncaster that year; Spike Judd, Wizz, Deb, Dave Russell and I watched Frenzy, The Business, Potato 5, Desmond Dekker and Bad Manners, where we all had a mini moment of fame when a poster with photos from the 1986 rallies was produced where we all are slap bang in the middle, sat in front of the stage soaking up the atmosphere. This inland rally also held a big custom show in the main building and there was a very tightly packed campsite. But because of the new restrictions in 1987, there were no more nighttime dos put on

At MSC Open Day 1987

or bands to be seen on the rallies, so if live music was the choice, places like The Pink Toothbrush were where you had to go.

If not a custom show, then there were often dealers such as Bedlam Scooters and Midland Scooter Centre (MSC) that would put on open days to tempt you to part with your hard-earned cash and maybe purchase one of the new Vespa T5s or P125ETS's, the latest go-faster goodies or some shiny chrome plated bolt on parts. The MSC open day was a busy one, if it had been a ticketed event then it would definitely have been a sell-out. The surrounding area thronged with scooterists, and the streets rang with the sound of two stroke engines, just like a mini scooter rally. I dread to think what Norrie Kerr and Dave Webster, the owners of MSC as well as seasoned engine tuners and scooter racers in their own right, thought (let alone the local residents) of all the people that were rammed into their shop begging to hand over cash for scooter parts, but I do know that they were both revered then as they still are now. In fact, I couldn't believe it years later when I was out on a racetrack at the same time as Norrie Kerr, who was thoroughly enjoying himself even if he wasn't leading the pack as he would have been some 40 years earlier.

Great Yarmouth was my first rally that year, cadging a lift on the back of Jonny's burgundy Vespa P200E, fitted with Yankee seat and possibly a Pitone exhaust, but the quieter baffled version. If it had been the baffle-less version, I certainly would have remembered the ear-splitting noise that the exhaust was renowned for. Jonny was always generous providing me with a lift on his scooter when needed, but he had a distracting habit of eyeing up the girls while riding along. When I was on the back of his scooter it was always a worry that one day, riding through Cambridge city centre in the summer, these distractions would get the better of him and crash, bang, wallop, we would find ourselves forcibly implanted into the rear bumper of the car we were following. Thankfully, he was paying full attention when our group were pulled into the police roadblock for security checks and searches though. The atmosphere at Great Yarmouth was subdued compared to previous rallies and the main topic of conversation would have been how the rallies continued and when or if evening entertainment would make a return. Thankfully, things would return to normal eventually.

The Isle of Wight still held a rally in '87 but it was moved to an earlier date over the Whitsun weekend to try and deter troublemakers. Again, the ride down was overnight, and this added to the sense of adventure that these times held. I had got hold of a nice little Vespa Primavera and rode that to the rally with Dwain. We set off down the A10, treating ourselves to a Little Chef meal en route, before heading towards London and weaving our way through the metropolis to pick up the A3 towards Portsmouth. When we arrived on the island, the camp site was in Sandown and where we would meet up with everyone else from Cambridge. Years later, on a family holiday, I would take my children to see where the rally was held and try to describe it to them. I doubt that they could imagine at the time what I was talking about, but when we conveniently timed a family camping holiday with the rally, me on my scooter and them with their mum in the car, they then got to see for themselves what it was all about, even if it was a lot more civilised some 20+ years later, but they got the idea.

One year (possibly 1987?) there was a Hells Angels gathering on the island at the same time as the scooter rally and as far as I am aware there was no conflict between the two groups over the weekend. Thankfully, the old rivalries were beginning to be left behind with bikers appreciating how much time and money scooterists spent on their machines as well as the miles we put in on them and the fact that a lot of scooterists did their own repairs, often fixing the scooter by the side of the road when needed. We could appreciate their machines too. While having a good look over a bike parked outside the pub where we were drinking, its owner soon appeared to make sure we were not getting too close to it. We were wary of this biker even though we regularly drank in a biker pub in Cambridge (The Boat Race), admittedly this was partly for the supply of certain illicit items that some of our group would partake in, but we were soon all chatting away and talking about the two "same but different" takes on two wheels, even if ours were a lot smaller. This respect has continued to grow over the years and is mutual, but there are still many people, both motorcycle riders and "normal" people, that aren't aware of the mileage some scooter riders put in on these little machines that weren't really intended to go much further than the shops and who also view every scooter riding person as a parka wearing mod or a weekend hooligan.

L to R Trevor, Carl, Hannah and Shona

Carl with Trevor's cutdown propped against the wall

Exploring the island, we stopped off at Alum Bay and took the treetop skimming ski lift down to the beach where I have a couple of photos of us looking like we didn't have a care in the world, sprawled out on the pebble beach soaking up the sun. We resisted the urge to pay for the privilege of filling glass jars with the coloured sand found there, but we did splash out on a boat trip out to see the chalk stacks jutting into the sea, known as the Needles. They rise dramatically out of the waves with a lighthouse at the furthest point to warn local shipping of their presence. The group riding round the island was made up of me on my Primavera, Trevor Peat (now owner of Cambridge Lambretta Workshop), who had been persuaded to ride a friends bright yellow Vespa with her as pillion, and Carl Cartwright with girlfriend Hannah as pillion on his Lambretta.

Back in Cambridge, Trevor would normally be riding his lovely red and chrome cutdown Lambretta powered by an early TS1 kit alongside Carl, Trevor's best mate, who had been working hard on his white and chrome cutdown with extended forks to get it back on the road and ready for the rally. Carl's scooter was a good looking one, individual but subtle, even with its extended forks. It was unusual as, even though it had an obvious chopper influence due to the forks, it retained some of its bodywork which was tastefully trimmed and together with Trevor on his scooter, they would have caught many admiring glances from onlookers as they rode round the streets of Cambridge.

MILES AND MILES AND MILES

So far in my scooter riding life, the journeys had been quite near, the furthest rally being within 150 miles. However, this was soon to change with a much longer haul and my first excursion north of the border. I was without a roadworthy scooter; my little 125cc Primavera was not up to the job, and I really fancied going to the Scottish rally in June. During a conversation in the pub with a mate, Brian Gourley, it turned out that he would be willing to be the pillion on his own scooter, a standard Vespa P150X, while I rode it the 400 or so miles up to Girvan on the west coast of Ayrshire and back again. I had recently passed my motorcycle test to obtain a full licence on the day before my provisional licence ran out, narrowly avoiding a two-year compulsory loss of licence and could now legally carry a pillion passenger. I passed despite, throughout the test, not being able to select neutral on my little Primavera when the examiner signalled me to stop and I'm sure I skidded on the emergency stop exercise too, perhaps he felt sorry for me or had to get his pass quota up for that week? Who knows? These were the days when the test route was no more the 500 yards from the test centre. The examiner would walk up to meet you where he would give you his instructions which would be along the lines of "keep turning left (or right) until you arrive back here" and there were often stories to be heard of test candidates falling off their bike out of sight of the examiner, remounting and still successfully passing their test because of the blind spots!

The rally soon arrived, and we were keen to get going on our way up north that Friday night in June 1987. I don't think either of us really appreciated how far an 800-mile round trip, two up on a modestly powered Vespa with no back rest or home comforts would be, but we soon found out. Heading west across the A45 to pick up the M6 for the trudge north in the middle of June, we had the advantage of long hours of daylight and made good progress before darkness fell. The further north we travelled the bigger the crowds of scooters were at the petrol stations in the northbound motorway services. Approaching the forecourt to refuel was quite daunting with everyone's gaze turning on us as we pulled in, but once we removed our crash helmets it wasn't long before someone would ask where we came from or how the ride was going and this all added to the buzz of

Nearly there, on the way to Girvan

heading to a rally, particularly when it was such a trek. Having headed this far north, it was also difficult not to be impressed by the distances that the Scottish scooterists had to travel to reach their destination in England, rally after rally. Approaching the border into Scotland, I pulled over onto the motorway hard shoulder and made the obligatory but illegal stop next to the "Welcome to Scotland" sign for some photographs, but hey-ho we were scooterboys on a mission, so we cocked a snook to the authorities and snapped away.

The M6 became the Scottish A74(M) which we soon left to head through Gretna Green and then on toward Dumfries on the A75. Despite it supposedly being flaming June, the temperatures in those early hours of the day were fresh, but to be riding along, looking ahead at the rolling countryside, and seeing the tarmac disappear into blankets of white and then ride down into the morning mist that we had just been looking at, was quite surreal. From Dumfries, it was only a couple of hours of riding to reach Girvan and our anticipation was building. This, along with the roads that swept and flowed through the hilly countryside approaching the coast, meant that I was enjoying the ride more and more and our speed was increasing, until that is, I felt a tap on my shoulder followed by Brian politely but firmly instructing me to "slowdown!" It was his scooter so only right that I did as I was told. Obediently I eased off the throttle and relaxed for the last few miles towards Girvan. We found the campsite at around six or seven in the morning, rode through the gate into the field and parked up as we revelled in the achievement of reaching our first long distance rally in one piece and with the whole weekend ahead of us.

Before heading to Girvan, Dwain's dad (who was a lorry driver), warned me about some of the Scottish police, particularly those from Glasgow, who were renowned for being a tough and unforgiving lot and who might be shipped into police the rally. He wasn't wrong in the policing style, from what we were told when we bumped into some of the Rat & Rodents SC later that morning. Someone from the Huntingdon Ratshaggers SC was enjoying a beer somewhere in the town, when the beer glass slipped through his hand smashing onto the pavement. He was quickly arrested for being drunk and disorderly and dragged off to spend the day in a cell to "sober up". I must point out, that I may or may not have the scooter clubs mentioned the wrong way round but, in my defence, it was 36 years ago.

Even with the drastic consequences of any behaviour deemed as loutish or unacceptable by the police, we headed to the pub to take advantage of the Scottish all day licencing hours, which we were not yet able to enjoy south of the border and take advantage of it we did. Too much, too soon, on too little food and with too little sleep soon meant we were both well and truly drunk, fit for nothing but having a great time, and Brian found himself worshipping the porcelain gods in the gents' toilets before too long. Thankfully, this must have got rid of much of the alcohol in his systems as quickly as it entered. We then headed out into the refreshing outdoors in search of food, sustenance, and the campsite, feeling as if we had enjoyed only one or two civilised pints rather than the quantity we actually had.

It was late afternoon when we were wondering what the plan was going to be for the evening. I'm not sure who mentioned it first, Brian or me, but it suddenly dawned on us that if it had taken 12 hours to reach Girvan then it would take at least another 12 hours to make the return journey and we needed to be fit for work on Monday morning, which was a tall order at that moment. The decision was made, we were heading home despite the alcohol that we had consumed. Looking back, there is no way I would now consider setting off having just spent lunch time in the pub. It was a reckless and naïve decision. We both felt ok and in control, partly due to our youthful ignorance so we packed our gear onto the scooter, donned our thankfully full face crash helmets and set off. The gate leaving the campsite had a few police officers standing guard who thankfully waved us through as we held our breathe and crossed our fingers. With relief at not being collared by them, I eased the Vespa out onto the road and pointed the scooter homeward.

The return ride on the A Roads leaving Girvan was more sedate this time and we eventually found our way onto the motorway to start the plod south. Once darkness fell and we were riding along the motorway, we both started to feel tired following our overindulgence earlier in the day. Brian was at risk of falling asleep and off the back of the seat and I was at risk of closing my sleepy eyes and stuffing both machine and riders into a field by the side of the carriageway or worse. In fact, two or three times I had closed my eyes briefly to open them again to find we were veering dangerously onto the hard shoulder. Realising the risk of our stupidity, we made regular stops at motorway service stations where we would find a table, sit down and drop straight off to sleep. This pattern of riding was continued through the night; ride, get tired, park up and sleep, but somehow, we got through the night without being stopped by the police and breathalysed, killing ourselves or worse still, killing someone else. The ride was slow and relentless and the monotony of the M6 did not help, but eventually we arrived home in Cambridge some 24 hours after our departure. The journey time worked out at an average of about 17 miles an hour, shockingly slow. We arrived home thoroughly knackered after our longest trip so far, but both had one question in our heads... where next?

DEFECTIVE BREAKDOWN

If it wasn't a rally weekend, there would occasionally be a custom show to visit where we could get a close look at some of the top machines of the day. We visited one of the Trent Custom Shows, another put on by the Oxford Roadrunners SC and the LCGB Super Custom Show at the Queensway Hall in Dunstable. The standard and variety of machines at these shows was outstanding and the owners were able to show their scooters off to their best with themed back drops and enhancing lights, having spent hours polishing paintwork and chrome plating before putting them on display. We would drift around the hall admiring concourse standard restorations, cutdowns, street racers, choppers, extensively muralled mobile works of art and fantastically engineered scooters.

Even back then the scooters must have cost a small fortune, the chrome plating and engraving that was often seen on what started off as very humble little machines, would need to be sourced from specialist companies or craftsmen with immense skill then put together carefully whilst trying not to scratch the lusciously lacquered paintwork. I never saw myself owning a machine that would be worthy of displaying at a custom show, so I was content to gaze longingly at the scooters that were there and, like lifelong favourite records bought as a teenager, would stay in my mind as the scooters that others would forever be judged by, scooters like Spirit Walker, Sign of the Snake, Illusion, Sweeter Than Wine, Worlds Apart, Future Shock, a DTC racer or the fantasy art influenced Vespa Mytho Poeikon (however it was pronounced), to name but a few.

On the way to a Custom Show

Queensway Hall Dunstable
Tel. 0582 603326
Fri. 20th
Sept. 7.45
KING
KURT
+ MATTHEWS BROTHER
Bar Free Parking
Tickets from Box Office, F.L. Moores, Record City Luton, Davids Bookshop Letchworth
Classical Rock Harpenden, Spiders Webb, Zodiac St. Albans.
B & A Bletchley, Buzzard Leighton Buzzard, E.G.E. St. Albans Rd. Watford tel 42493,
Earth Records Aylesbury Old Town Records Hemel OR ON THE DOOR
CHEQUES PAYABLE TO SPORTS & LEISURE LTD ONLY WITH SAE.
(Rats and Rodents 50p off on door only)

SEETHROUGH TOUR 86
15th Aberdeen Victoria
16th Chester Angels
19th Colchester Works
20th Carlisle Stars & Stripes
21st Hull Adelphi

SCOOTER RIDER
THE OFFICIAL MAGAZINE
OF THE
NATIONAL SCOOTER RIDERS ASSOCIATION
24

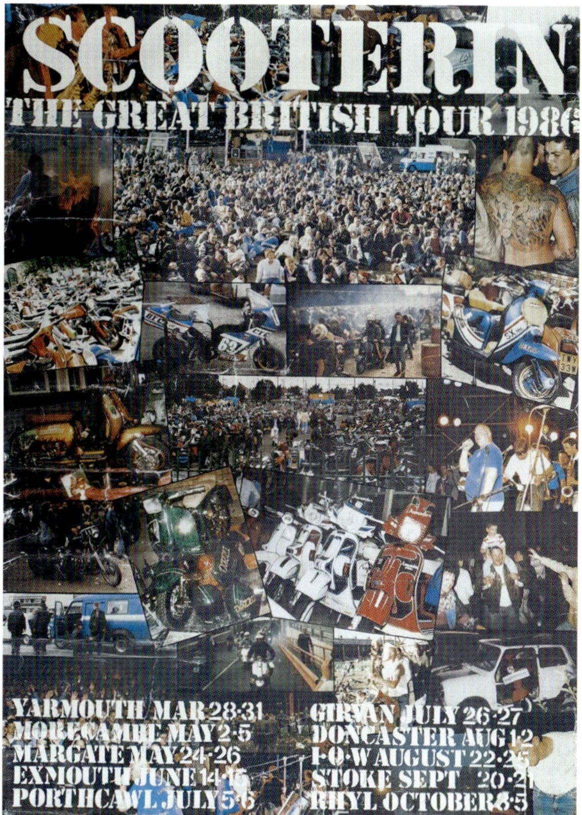
SCOOTERIN
THE GREAT BRITISH TOUR 1986
YARMOUTH MAR 28·31
MORECAMBE MAY 2·5
MARGATE MAY 24·26
EXMOUTH JUNE 14·15
PORTHCAWL JULY 5·6
GIRVAN JULY 26·27
DONCASTER AUG 1·2
I·O·W AUGUST 22·25
STOKE SEPT 20·21
RHYL OCTOBER 3·5
©1986 ALIEN CO-OPERATIVE

At that time, the closest I did get to a custom scooter were two smart machines that were well put together and quite individual but not built by myself. The Lambretta TV225 cutdown was past its best when I first bought it. It was still a good looking machine but needed a rebuild to restore it to its former glory after I had put some miles on it, and bits had broken off or rattled loose from the vibrations. It was duly stripped down and put into boxes with the intention of getting it back together again soon. What I didn't appreciate at the time was how much money this sort of project could soak up, particularly when my lowly wage could not realistically fund it and, at that time, my mechanical knowledge and ability did not really match the ideas in my head. About four or five years later I did have the frame repainted British racing green (and unoriginally named Pretty Green) by Nick Jolly at Surrey & Hants Scooters and Mark Broadhurst at MB Developments built the engine as a Stage 3 Honda 205cc conversion, but that was as far as I got at the time. So back into boxes it went, to be carried into and then out of removal vans when we moved house, but always with the intention of getting it back on the road at some point.

The other scooter wasn't a custom scooter as such, just a gorgeous Vespa Rally cutdown built by an older Cambridge scooterist who I can only remember as Dave. Again, knowing I needed to get mobile (I did spend a fair bit of time off the road back then), a mutual friend put me onto this scooter. Seeing it was like a premonition of the guitar shop scene in the (yet to be shot) film Waynes World where in awestruck rapture Wayne proclaims, "It will be mine, oh yes, it will be mine". There were two Andys, who were also best mates, involved in the rise and fall of this scooter, Andy Lindsay (now owner of Mod Shoes online shop) who introduced me to Dave and the scooter, and Andy Cunningham who was present at the start of its quick and sad demise not long after.

The Vespa Rally has a bit of a cult following and was known for being the predecessor of the later and less classically styled Vespa P Range. In its standard form the engine was quite quick, a real mile muncher and the scooter was an aptly named rally machine. I always felt it looked a little wide and portly compared to earlier Vespas, the rear end always looked like it was carrying a lot of weight and appeared quite low slung to me. Please don't shoot me if you are a Rally devotee, I like them I just don't think they were as svelte as other models. However, this Rally was different. It couldn't be called portly as it didn't wear any side panels so was only half dressed. The lack of panels showed off a bright yellow powder coated engine casing and chromed flywheel cover on one side and a spare wheel and on the other. The frame was painted with a well applied coating of gunmetal grey Hammerite paint, and the hubs were powder coated in the contrasting yellow. This combination of grey, yellow and chrome, worked brilliantly, but what really set the scooter off, grabbing my attention and giving it a special look, was its poise. The rear end was trimmed upwards exposing more of the rear tyre than normal, while at the front a pair of Lambretta GP handlebars gave me something to hold onto while sticking my elbows out wide and a two-tone grey sports seat provided somewhere to stretch back into, scooterboy-style. It looked good, if not being a position I could hold for prolonged periods without my back giving me grief. Along with a set of Lambretta forks, a minimalist mudguard and disc brake hub, the front end of the scooter had a look of solidity and purpose missing from a standard Vespa Rally and most importantly, it looked like a proper scooterboy's scooter. I didn't have a lot of luck with this scooter sadly and my ownership was short-lived.

However, having got it I just wanted to get out and ride my new scooter, so the day after I bought it, I gave my younger brother a lift to work on it. Off we went two up through a village where there was a railway level crossing. Despite slowing down for the anticipated bumps, as the road sloped down towards the tracks then levelled out, the rear suspension bottomed out forcing the number plate onto the rear tyre, bending it upwards and knocking the rear light out of its housing. Next, when riding down the M11 to the Margate rally with Jonny, Tom, and Dave of the Desert Rats, I saw some scooters up ahead, one of which was Andy Cunningham from Cambridge. Thinking it would be a good idea to catch up with them, I dropped down a gear and snapped the throttle open, leaving my group in a wake of two-stroke smoke. I caught up with the other group quickly and was just drawing alongside Andy to give him a wave, when the engine locked up solidly at over 60mph leaving a streak of tyre rubber on the tarmac and my heart in my mouth. The scooter's rear end swung to the left and then the right as it skidded along while all I could do was pull the clutch in, aim for the hard shoulder and hope that I reached it upright. Suddenly

Desert Rats SC at Margate 1987

there was a gaggle of scooters on the hard shoulder wondering what the hell had just happened, particularly Andy and myself, and shock became piss-taking, at my expense, as we tried to work out what had happened.

My memory is a blur from here. Whether the scooter engine freed itself and started up again so that I could ride the rest of the way or whether some passing members of the Paralytics SC stopped and put the scooter in their van, taking it onto Margate while I jumped on the back of Jonny's scooter, I'm not sure. But I do recall stripping the clutch down outside the B&B in Margate to find that the thrust washer, a vital part of the clutch, had partially broken. I had a bit of a cob on for a bit, because of the breakdown, but this was resolved with a few beers that evening before the Paralytics SC support van took my broken scooter back to Cambridge for me and dropped it home where I could replace the offending thrust washer and get riding again.

Riding the Vespa a few weeks later up to the Scarborough rally with Brian and heading north along the A1, we had just passed Peterborough when the scooter's engine died forcing us to pull over onto a footpath. With our limited expertise, we couldn't get any life back into the scooter, so the decision was made to call the RAC out. Not really wanting to miss the rally and despite the traumatic ride to Girvan and back, poor Brian either offered or allowed me to ride his scooter again with him as pillion. We had to wait for the breakdown recovery to arrive and when it did the scooter was loaded up onto the recovery lorry, drop off instructions were given, and it was driven back home under a cloud of shame. We continued our journey north to meet up with the rest of the Desert Rats. Eventually arriving at Scarborough and meeting up with the rest of the club, we headed into town and found a pub to start the evening. We must have been waiting to get a drink in the first pub for all of two minutes before we were unceremoniously told by the landlord to leave by the door we came in through. No one knew what had been said to cause offence, least of all Tom who had been the focus of the landlord's angst, but we retreated to search out another pub. Whether it was because we were southerners, scooter riders or to make things worse, southern scooter riders, we didn't

Paralytics and Desert Rats at Margate

know and we did not have any luck finding a hospitable pub after that, so we returned to our hotel to make use of the resident's bar late into the night creating a hangover from hell for the next day, a definite "I'm never drinking again" hangover, at least not until the following weekend.

Following that rally, unsuccessful attempts were made to bring the scooter back to life but sadly all in vain. It was taken apart down the side of Mum and Dads house, put back together and then taken apart again when that didn't work. Frustration grew and despite all my efforts, I was not to get it running again. The scooter was sold off bit by bit until it was no more, and I was left dejected and scooterless again as the rally season came to an end. The approaching winter was dark and cold, both literally and figuratively, it being the year that Dwain was involved in his fatal crash. Part of youth's innocence and one of my childhood friends was lost to me that year. His death had a profound effect on me that has stayed with me all these years. Life is short, nobody knows what is round the corner and it made me realise that sometimes you need to release your grip and go with the flow.

Heading home in the Paralytics SC support van, Margate 1987

LONDON GIRL

It's 1988, I am 19 years old with no real idea of where my life was taking me. I had no real plans, apart from trying to keep a scooter on the road that is reliable enough to get me to the next scooter rally and back with the little money that I had to my name. Losing a friend so needlessly and so suddenly could have made anyone lose the plot and go off the rails, it was a lot to deal with at that young age. Thankfully for me, after the initial shock it had a positive effect. It made me throw caution to the wind a little bit more than before and confirmed the old adage that you only get one go in this world, life is not a practice run. Clichéd, but true.

Sat in the pub on a Friday night with the usual scooter crowd, I'm catching up with friends, having a laugh and topping up the Greene King IPA levels in my blood when a girl stood at the bar catches my eye. Like most teenagers, I'm keen to find a girl to partner up with, call my girlfriend and spend time with, who knows, maybe even make family plans with, but this girl doesn't look like she would be part of the scooter scene, let alone even look at a crew cut, beer swilling scooterboy whose only plan that night was to keep the beer flowing and pick up a pizza on my way home from the legendary Cambridge late night institution Colonel Fudpuckers. I turn away, take a sup of beer from my glass, and think no more of her.

A few minutes pass until I sense someone sit down on the stool next to me. Bloody hell it's her, sat next to me. What do I do? "Oh hello" I say, as my brain tries to compute the situation; boy sees girl, boy thinks girl looks nice but doesn't know what to do, boy carries on with beer and life, but then… It turns out she is the sister of Jackie, a friend and club mate, and she has been dragged into town for the night to meet Jackie's scooter friends. Her name is Lesley and, despite my attempts at conversation and humour, we get on well. Don't despair though, this is not a Mills & Boon story and I'm not going to put you through the story of how things developed from that night in the Rose & Crown, apart from, we ended up going out together, I moved down to London so that we could live together, get married and bring four great children into the world. We were together over 30 years, sharing life's ups and downs, good times and bad times, before it was time to go our separate ways.

Throughout all those years, scooters were a constant presence, whether it was buying a nice cheap and reliable but slow Vespa 150 Sprint to get me to London and back to visit my new girlfriend, transferring the boxed up Lambretta cutdown onto the removal van yet again or being told that there was another box of scooter parts delivered for me, followed by the accusatory and questioning "Can you afford all these bits Mark?" They only cost 20 quid, honest.

The 150 Sprint was bought from club mate David Childs, who also happened to be going out with Lesley's sister Jackie at the time, so I got it for a very reasonable price, cheers Dave. Painted black, it looked good but was a bit of a plodder due to the standard engine. Overtaking juggernauts on the M11 had to be timed correctly, on a downhill stretch of motorway or with some nifty slipstreaming to get a slingshot past the bigger vehicle. Going to work, a couple of months later, I was knocked off it by a car driver turning in front of me while I was filtering, and the scooter was written off by the insurance company. Deciding I needed something reliable and with a bit more power, the money I received from the insurance claim went towards another scooter, F300 NEB, a brand new Vespa PX200 EFL in black, that I picked up on the 1st of August 1988. My first new scooter since the PK50 four years earlier was funded by a loan, with Dad as the guarantor again, and was a big moment for me. Whilst not the most exciting scooter, I would say the PX was the mainstay of the rally scene around that time, being available to buy from new and with its generally bullet-proof engine, in standard form that is, and mine lived up to that reputation. It would take me up and down the motorway to London two or three times a week for many months with the throttle held back against the stop wherever possible. Its top speed was helped or hindered by the direction of the wind or how much traffic there was to give me a helping tow, pulling me along in its wake. I would also drag it up and down the country to meet my Cambridge mates at whatever rally was taking place, often riding solo from London and going until the fuel gauge was nearing empty when I would stop to fill up, have a quick drink and then get cracking again.

BEYOND THE THRESHOLD

I moved down to London to live with Lesley at the end of 1988 and after a couple of years got myself a job as a motorcycle instructor with a company called CSM Rider Training. During some of the 5 years of working for them I had the use of a company motorcycle, so when I had to sell F300 NEB I still thankfully had two wheeled transport and was able to choose between bikes such as a Kawasaki GT550, Suzuki GS500E, Honda 650 Revere or a Triumph Trident 750, very different to my little Vespa and was even able, on the sly, to take the Suzuki around the Brands Hatch race circuit for a track day, great fun! I used to take pride and enjoyment in the moment a student would occasionally ask what bike it was that I rode. In reply I would ask them something like "did you see the CBR1000 parked outside?" to which they would ask with wide open eyes "Wow, yes! Is that yours then?" and, with a twinkle in my eye, I would reply "No, mine's the Vespa parked next to it!" Working as an instructor, guiding up to five learner riders along the busy roads of South East London with only a one-way radio and a set of mirrors to keep an eye on the group behind me, was a great experience. I met some fantastic people as both students and fellow instructors and used to enjoy thrashing my scooter around the South Circular Road with them on the way home after work. It did get to the point though where I was riding my scooter too much like a motorcycle though and had to satisfy the need for speed with my very own Suzuki RGV250M for a while. The experience of riding what was effectively a 250cc two-stroke race bike with lights and a number plate was phenomenal, and being able to outride a larger bike on the right type of road was such a buzz, and one that I am so glad I experienced, but I have to say that however much fun it was, it didn't come with the rallies, camaraderie and experiences that riding a scooter all around the UK and Europe has given me over the years.

The engine on my PX was kept standard, apart from the exhaust, and the only additions made were a cradle back rest and a flat rear carrier. After a couple of years, I had an attempt at spraying some logos of punk band Stiff Little Fingers onto the bodywork, one of my favourite bands then and now. Around that time, we would see them quite a few times live, so using them on the scooter was fitting. The Inflammable Material flame logo was used on the side panels and a Rigid Digit logo on the toolbox door. It was

SUMMONS
CAMBRIDGE MAGISTRATES COURT 1165

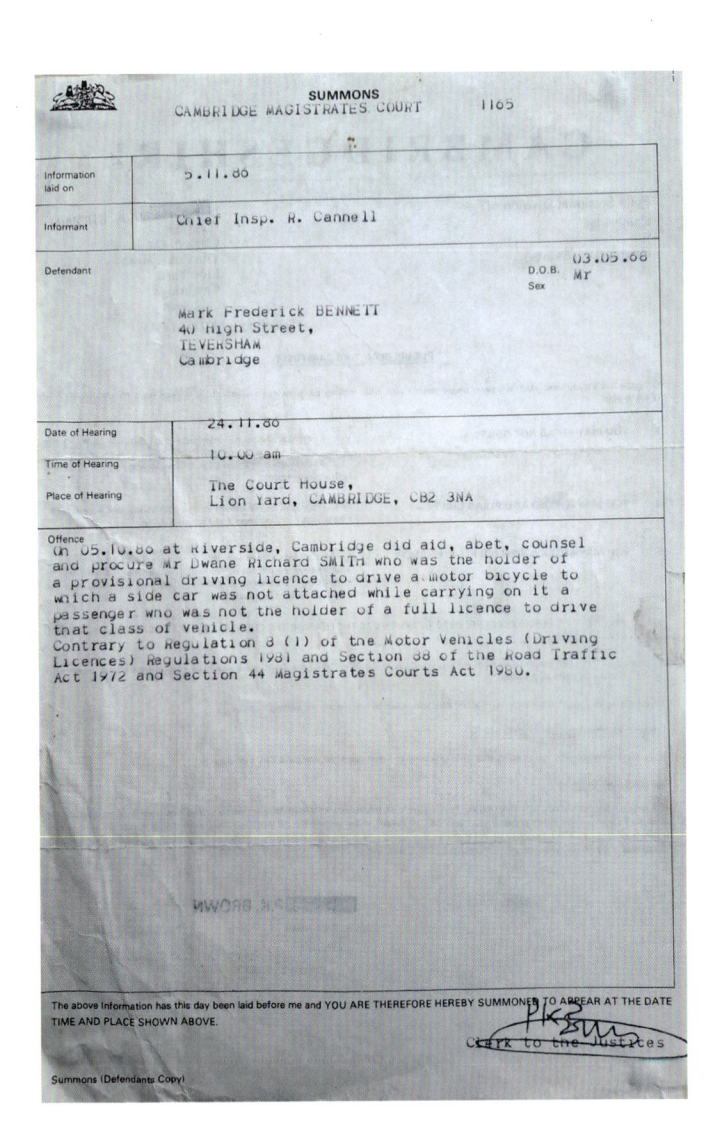

Information laid on	5.11.80
Informant	Chief Insp. R. Cannell
Defendant	Mark Frederick BENNETT 40 High Street, TEVERSHAM Cambridge
D.O.B.	03.05.68
Sex	Mr
Date of Hearing	24.11.80
Time of Hearing	10.00 am
Place of Hearing	The Court House, Lion Yard, CAMBRIDGE, CB2 3NA

Offence
On 05.10.80 at Riverside, Cambridge did aid, abet, counsel and procure Mr Dwane Richard SMITH who was the holder of a provisional driving licence to drive a motor bicycle to which a side car was not attached while carrying on it a passenger who was not the holder of a full licence to drive that class of vehicle.
Contrary to Regulation 8 (1) of the Motor Vehicles (Driving Licences) Regulations 1981 and Section 88 of the Road Traffic Act 1972 and Section 44 Magistrates Courts Act 1980.

The above Information has this day been laid before me and YOU ARE THEREFORE HEREBY SUMMONED TO APPEAR AT THE DATE TIME AND PLACE SHOWN ABOVE.

Clerk to the Justices

Summons (Defendants Copy)

You're nicked sonny Jim!

NSRA membership card from 1990

The Bats SC road trial route booklet

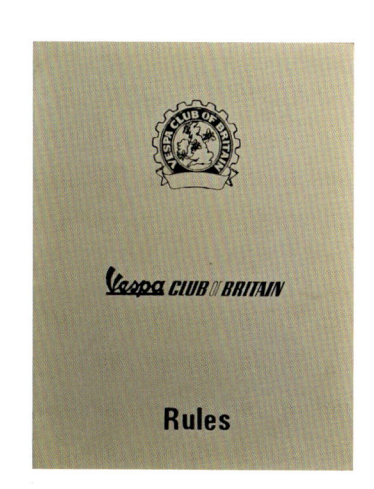

89

far from a professional job, the edges weren't as sharp as I'd have liked, as I had left the stencils and masking tape on too long, but it was my own work which set it apart from any other standard PX on a rally campsite and from a distance, it looked great.

It earned its keep, being ridden relentlessly all year round and often two-up loaded with luggage. Once I even strapped the cutdown's Lambretta engine to its back seat and rode up to MB Developments near Doncaster, dropping it off for them to rebuild it. I dread to count the number of times I rode that scooter up and down the M11 between London and Cambridge and, during the first winter, it wasn't unusual to arrive at work with a coating of ice on the front of my jacket and frozen eyebrows, despite layering up until I looked like the Michelin man, and it would be well into the afternoon until I thawed out.

Riding so much on motorways at that time, it was inevitable that I would see the results of the occasional crash and even though they are statistically safe roads, when things go wrong, they go wrong in style. On one occasion, I had just ridden under the M25 interchange towards London. On this stretch I would often take advantage of the downhill section of carriageway, riding up close to the lorry in its slipstream for a few moments before pinning the throttle and shooting past, hoping I would gain enough speed to break the solid wall of air that is often met when drawing level with the drivers cab (these were the days before HGVs were limited to 57mph). That day it was raining quite hard, so I had decided to stay back where I was and thank goodness I did. Where I would normally time my overtake, the lorry I was following suddenly and inexplicably jack-knifed while doing about 60 to 65mph. My heart stopped as I watched the lorry's cab swing out to a right-angle to its trailer and into the middle lane. As the driver wrestled with the steering wheel, the lorry headed for the central reservation just missing it as the whole cab swung onto full lock in the opposite direction, recrossing both lanes to the left before crossing the hard shoulder, heading up the embankment and crashing through a wooden fence, finally coming to a stop in the field with barely six feet of the trailer left hanging over the embankment. On another day, I saw the front wheel of a HGV detach from its axle and do an admirable impression of a bouncing bomb as it overtook the vehicles in front, somehow avoiding them all before heading for the hard shoulder and coming to a stop. Both drivers would have been dumbstruck by what had happened to them and were lucky to come out of their close escapes scratch free. It certainly taught me to be ready for the unexpected and to be grateful for arriving at a destination safe and sound.

Some 37,000 miles of hard riding were clocked up on F300 NEB's speedo before it suffered a major engine failure. It was rebuilt by Surrey & Hants Scooters so that I could continue racking up the miles and as well as all the riding in the UK, it was taken over to France twice for touring holidays. Fully loaded on the front and rear of the scooter, and with motorcycle courier panniers borrowed from an instructor mate slung over the side panels, we headed in the direction of the Loire valley on the first trip. Camping throughout, we were lucky to enjoy unbroken sunshine and quiet French country roads, while taking full advantage of the local cuisine and wine.

The following year when we travelled around Brittany and Normandy, the weather was the complete opposite and made the camping experience so much harder. I struggled with constantly packing and unpacking wet camping gear and was not the happy travelling companion of the previous year. Sadly, I was expecting a repeat of the previous year's weather, which did not happen, and on the one dry and sunny day of the trip Lesley was adamant she was going to sit on the beach and top up her suntan. Sitting for an entire day on the beach was difficult and made me restless, disturbing the calm Lesley was hoping to enjoy, and to top it all I got sunburnt! How we would laugh (?) retelling the stories of our trips to the kids as they grew older.

Closer to home in South East London, it wasn't unusual to bump into other scooterists and get chatting, whether it was pulling up at the same bike parking bay, at Kickstart Scooters on a Saturday afternoon or, while out shopping, recognising a fellow rally-goer by their flight jacket, badges, and Paddy Smith patches. It wouldn't be unusual to then bump into them again somewhere on a rally and restart the conversation.

I got to know the South East London Bats SC around that time too. They met regularly in nearby Greenwich. Barry and Rose Baker were the mainstay of the club at the time along with Cosa owning Pete, Steve who wrote a scooter off in a collision with a horse or a big deer, Geoff Mason (builder of the Guiness Custom Lambretta) and Norah, and Paul from Northern Ireland. As well as attending the national rallies, The Bats were a big part of the old-style scooter sport scene, organising and taking part in events such as road trials, treasure hunts, grass-tracking and off-road trials.

The first event I took part in with them was a treasure hunt that started down on the south coast at Birling Gap. This event consisted of following brief directions made up of icons and abbreviated instructions indicating which exit to take at a roundabout or which direction to turn at a T-Junction for example, whilst at the same time identifying landmarks or answering set questions to gain points along the way. It sounds easy enough, everyone sets off separately with timed gaps, and follows the same plan, but despite everyone having the same set of instructions, I remember seeing several scooters all approach a check point from different directions on more than one occasion. Then there would be some good-humoured competition, maybe involving sending the others in the wrong direction or sharing incorrect answers to keep people on their toes. Old-fashioned fun that gave a good reason to get out and ride a scooter around some lovely roads and scenic countryside. I think I came second in that event and went on with Steve to win the Oxford Roadrunners SC 100 Road Trial, which The Bats were quite chuffed with to say the least, getting one over the Roadrunners, and it gave us an impressive trophy to look after for a year too. These were very different ways of enjoying scooters to what I was used to on a national rally, where the campsite could resemble a sea of army green with all the practical and hard wearing clothing worn to go to somewhere like Morecambe, but a Bats trip to the Vespa Club of Britain (VCB) AGM entailed putting on a suit and hob-nobbing with highly regarded VCB grown-ups such as Charles Caswell and Norrie Kerr. It certainly wasn't a sober affair though, as the landlady of our B&B could testify after I was sick in the night, and pebble dashed the bathroom, highly embarrassing when we checked out the next morning. These were just different sorts of nights out compared to a rally, but still meeting new people and having fun, all adding to the great big melting pot that is scootering.

In 6 years of ownership, I clocked up over 75,000 miles on F300 NEB, travelling around the country, to rallies, backwards and forwards to London and of course the two trips across the Channel and into France. It had an engine rebuild and a full respray, which was brought about after losing grip and low-siding it when trying to ride too quickly around a roundabout, before, along with the Suzuki RGV250, it was sold in 1994 for only five or six hundred pounds when the first of four children was about to make an appearance in our lives. As with so many people at that stage in life, finances and a new family member were the priority. I wish I had been able to hold onto to it, but I was crap at managing my money and not having any funds in reserve meant I could not keep it. A bike from work would provide the transport I needed, and the memories gained during my time of ownership were priceless.

Vespa PX bill of sale and owner's booklet

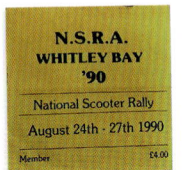

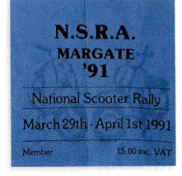

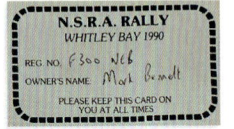

PART 2

DAWNING OF A NEW ERA...

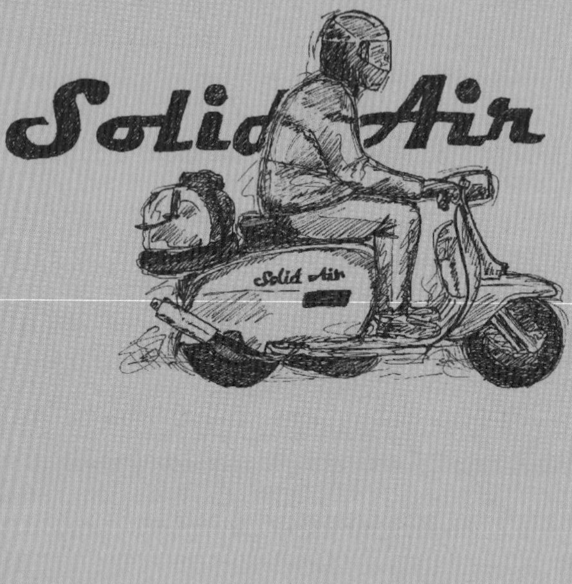
Solid Air
Solid Air

EXPRESS YOURSELF

I had not had a scooter on the road since I sold my PX200. A growing family took main stage and for a few years I lived and worked in the same village so two wheeled transport was not a necessity. There had still been scooter rallies taking place during that time but with lower numbers in attendance, they were soon to take off again though with a resurgence of interest in scooters and it was always my intention to get the cutdown rebuilt again. Issues of Scootering Magazine kept me in touch with the scene and provided small snippets of inspiration and, by pure chance, I had also ended up living next to fellow Desert Rats SC member Dave Childs for a few years. He still had and used his Vespa T5 and Spanish Lambretta Li150. I had picked up an old Indian GP with the intention of getting it roadworthy. Sadly, that did not stay for long as it needed too much attention, otherwise translated as "too much money throwing at it," which I could not justify at the time. But, with the cutdown biding its time whilst nestled in boxes in the garage, scooter pictures to pore over behind the locked door of a bathroom while seeking refuge from four young children, a fellow scooter enthusiast to chat with next door and, for a short period, a broken scooter whetting my appetite to get riding again, it wasn't going to be long before there would be the familiar two-stroke put put sound coming from a scooter that belonged to me that I could put through its paces and rekindle the feelings that had been put to one side for a few years.

A change of jobs found me training to work in the Operating Theatres at Addenbrookes Hospital in Cambridge. With it came an increased wage once I had qualified and a much more substantial journey to work than the previous two minute roll down the hill on my bicycle. The penny dropped; this surely must be the time for me to rebuild the cutdown? I had all the main parts of the bodywork; the engine had been built some years earlier by Mark Broadhurst as a stage 3 Honda 205cc conversion and was complete apart from an exhaust. All that was needed was a paintjob, a new seat, some fresh tyres and few bits and bobs to complete the job, in theory. Of course, like any rebuild project, be it a scooter, house or classic car, the final amount of money needed to complete the job was more than predicted, but far less than had it been a full-bodied scooter I justified to my long-suffering wife. I'd like to say that she good-humouredly put up with me and my excitement in anticipation of getting back on a scooter, but I don't think she really felt the joy as much as I did.

After 15 years or so, the cutdown was back on the road. It had been painted by Steve Allan from Newmarket, another scooter rider and member of the Paralytics SC, and put together by me. The main colour was silver with a subtle metallic finish and the engine, updated AF Fresco exhaust and cowls were all satin black. Simple, effective, and functional. It was great to be riding a scooter again, even at running in speeds it would get me up early so that I could take the scenic route into work, clocking up the miles in preparation for giving the throttle a more meaningful twist to see what the engine was capable of. As can be expected on a new build, there were fastenings that would rattle lose and need retightening, with an added drop of Loctite to hopefully keep them in place, electrical connectors that would work themselves free depriving me of a headlight (normally at night too) and control cables that would need a bit of adjustment after bedding in. As the phrase goes, it was all part of the fun, and mistakes were made to be learnt from and hopefully not repeated. Once it was fully run in, the engine proved to be great fun and with a good turn of speed, it would surprise people as I shot along the right hand lane of the A14 near to where I lived. The Fresco exhaust, even though it sounded slightly different from those in the 1980s, had a crisp two-stroke sound to it which would only encourage me to hold the throttle open a touch longer on hard acceleration or to give it an extra blip on slowing down. It was like being an irresponsible teenager all over again.

Any excuse to be out on the scooter was taken. It was ridden to work at the hospital and into town if what I needed to buy could be stuffed into a pocket or a rucksack, cutdowns not being renowned for their practical carrying abilities. Dave told me about a Sunday morning scooter meet-up in Cambridge and I popped along there with him one day. Thinking it would be 1980s style scooterists with some people there I knew; I was surprised when we parked up by some of the mildly disgusted looks towards my scooter. Looking around there were some lovely and well-presented machines, but they all had more of a classic 1960s style and the owners looked of that time period too. Some of them (but not all) really didn't get the 1980s cutdown style of my scooter being old mods, and I felt a different vibe to that of scooterists of my generation, but it is variety that makes the scooter scene more vibrant than many other similar scenes, it's not about being the same as everyone else.

GOIN' DOWN SOUTH

Dave and I revisited the Isle of Wight Scooter Rally, him on his Li150 and me on the cutdown. We took the "traditional" route down from Cambridge, following the A10 south and into London. At one point Dave pulled over at the side of the road somewhere in north London and told me that he couldn't change gear. He pulled off the side panel only to find that the small circlip on top of the gearchange pivot had made a break for freedom and was nowhere to be seen. We searched our toolboxes and spares but found no replacement. We were at a loss as to what to do. Amid the hubbub of the busy high street area, with us and our scooters tucked against some railings separating us from the throng of pedestrians on one side and taxis shooting past us on the other, I suggested having a look on the roadside by the kerb for some sort of clip or piece of wire that could be fashioned to sit on top of the swivel to keep it in place. And so that is what happened, in true scooter rally bodge repair style we persuaded a strip of thin wire that we found to do the job required of getting Dave to the rally campsite, where we could buy a replacement from one of the scooter dealers there. We travelled onwards hoping that the wire would hold out, and left London behind to follow the A3 towards Portsmouth and the ferry bound for the Isle of Wight. On our arrival, it was great to see large numbers of scooters buzzing around the island, enjoying the sun and that sense of freedom feeling that being away for the weekend on a scooter gives. Setting up our tents at the campsite we felt straight back at home amongst all the other scooterists there for the weekend. Compared to the atmosphere of a 1980s rally, particularly the late 80s, the atmosphere had a very relaxed feel, with many people there now older, calmer and wiser. They were all there to have a good time, drink, dance and then head home, hopefully breakdown free. For some reason, Dave's gearchange circlip wasn't replaced, but the piece of wire found by the kerb somewhere in north London got Dave home and kept doing its job for at least another year before it was finally replaced with a proper clip!

After a couple of years of being ridden, for social, domestic, pleasure and commuting purposes, as the insurance companies call it, the cutdown was looking a bit tired and in need of some attention. Rather than just a retouching of the paintwork, I decided that a complete rebuild was called for but this time I would give it a smarter look with a few shiny and uprated parts. The basic lines of the scooter were spot on, and it was not unusual for it to be recognised from its early 1980s incarnation as it had such a distinctive look. Originally it was painted sky blue, with lots of shiny chrome, the British Racing Green version was never completed and the silver, whilst effective, didn't show the scooter off to its best, but I did not want to plaster it with acres of chrome plate either. I finally settled on a candy red scheme and Steve from Newmarket did a wonderful job of painting it again. I remember collecting it when Steve had finished his part, thanking him, and saying how good it looked but it wasn't until I unloaded it into the shed that I fully appreciated how good a job he had done. The red was beautifully deep and shiny with a subtle metallic sparkle. I had also asked him to stencil a Series 3 Lambretta side panel badge in silver onto the NSU front petrol tank, which worked really well. The frame, handlebars, rear hub, toolbox and both petrol tanks were all in red. To contrast the colour, all of the engine and its cowls, the forks, Kawasaki front dampers and both small sports mudguards were treated to a coat of satin black and to provide some highlights, without going over the top, the shiny bits were kept to the polished stainless wheel rims, the exhaust, front hydraulic disc brake (which replaced the totally ineffective standard disc brake), a small sprint rack that was fitted to the front of the fork tube and then a sprinkling of polished parts such as levers and the headlight rim. To top it off, upholsterer Andy Nixon beautifully covered a small café racer style seat that was a little different to the Snetterton seat that had been fitted up until then. However good it looked though, after a while it was absolute bloody agony to sit on and would leave me traumatised after riding it for much more than an hour or two. It did look the part though. I had achieved the look I was after, smart with a bit of sparkle but not over the top, a real eye-catcher. I had done a good job, too good maybe?

Freshly rebuilt, clean and shiny - 2007

Not long after completing the build, Margate was the venue for the National Rally. Dave and I headed south on what must be one of the most boring routes to a rally, down the M11 until joining the M25, follow that round and over the Dartford Crossing, then joining the A2 which becomes the M2 until turning onto the A299 and riding past where, in a TV episode of Only Fools and Horses - Jolly Boys Christmas Special, Del Boy and the gang stop at the Roman Galley pub where Denzil takes over coach driving duties, the official driver having enjoyed one too many shandies. I had hoped to enter my scooter into the rally custom show but as we had to ride down on the Saturday, by the time we had arrived the show had just finished. My scooter did attract attention from onlookers though as a small crowd gathered round to have a look and pass on some favourable comments. Back at home not long after, some subtle and some not so subtle comments from my wife were made suggesting that as the scooter was in such good condition, now would be the optimum time to sell it and hopefully get a fair price for it. I managed to hold out for a while. I had owned the scooter for 21 years by that time and really didn't want to part with it, but there was no way I could justify throwing any more money at it in the future after two rebuilds in a handful of years. Also, my kids were growing up and I really would like to give them lifts on the back of a scooter to school or round to their friends' houses, which on the cutdown was impossible. A difficult decision was made, and it was put up for sale on eBay. I watched as bids came in and the price rose. The reserve was reached then passed. With satisfaction at reaching a good price but sadness at having to let go of something that I had owned for so many years, it was soon not going to be mine any longer. The winning bid arrived in the last few seconds and the cutdown would soon be off to its new owner, who as it turned out, only lived a few miles away from where I did. He told me he had a similar scooter in his younger days and bought mine to relive those memories. He collected it and before a couple of weeks passed by, had polished it to within an inch of its life. He was an absolute stickler for detail and gave it a fantastic shine. Each owner after me changed various bits on it, making it their own, and that never bothered me as it was no longer mine. I built it for me, my taste and my style, but once I gave up ownership then it was up to the new keeper to do what they wanted. The last I heard; it had ended up in South East London, right on the doorstep of where I had lived some 30 years earlier and where it had been stored in boxes in a garage, always with the intention of one day getting it back on the road. My job was done.

WHERE DO WE GO FROM HERE?

The choice of a replacement for the cutdown was the good old Vespa PX200. Not a particularly exciting machine but I knew from experience that they were a solid and reliable workhorse, I just had to find a good second-hand one. I scoured eBay, the classifieds, and for sale sections on a couple of forums and found what looked like a tidy example a few hours' drive north on the A1. On arrival at the arranged time on a Saturday morning, the seller strangely wasn't there so could not show me the scooter himself. His wife opened the garage and let me pull the scooter out into the daylight. When I tried to start the scooter, it didn't want to cooperate. Eventually life spluttered from the engine but with the difficulty starting, the seller not being there and a few other niggles with the scooter that did not sit right, I declined the chance to buy and made a hasty exit. This was a big spanner in the works as the advert looked promising and I needed transport quickly with the cutdown gone. A few frantic phone calls were made home for info on one or two other scooters that I had been looking at and I headed to AF Rayspeed nearby as they may have or know of something for sale. Nothing was to be found there but thankfully home got back to me with the phone number of a scooter for sale in Scarborough and as it was only half an hour further along the A64 I made a call to the seller, hoping the scooter was still for sale. My luck was in, and the seller was home. I headed to the address given, while keeping an eye on the clock as I still had to get back to Cambridge for work and the first of three night shifts. As soon as the seller opened the garage, I could tell that the scooter looked promising. The dark blue paintwork was tidy, and the engine had not been started as my arrival was at such short notice. Thankfully it fired up easily and after a close look at the bodywork and quick test ride we agreed on a price. Soon enough my new scooter was loaded into the van, and I was heading back down south again after a hectic but finally successful trip.

As hoped for, this PX was a good buy. Many problem-free miles were clocked up riding around the country, apart from the odd broken cable and occasionally the HT cap would randomly pop off the spark plug, normally when the throttle was pinned open against the stop riding along a motorway and often when in the right hand lane. There was no rhyme or reason why this would happen and there wouldn't be any warning, the engine would just die as with the disconnection there was no spark igniting the fuel inside the engine. I would stick out my left arm hoping I could quickly shoot over to the hard shoulder where it would be a simple fix; panel off, plug cap back on and away I would go again. All very strange. The only major engine drama with it was one year at the Isle of Wight rally. About a mile along the road from the Smallbrook Stadium campsite I was waiting to pull out at a junction, I eased the clutch lever out to pull away but was met with a clunk followed by the scooter lurching forward and stalling. Not sure exactly what had happened but suspecting it was clutch related, and once I realised it was not going to be a quick fix, I pushed the scooter back to the campsite. There was a dealer on site that provided a repair service for rally goers, so not having that many tools with me (it being a Vespa!), I joined the queue and waited for someone to have a look to see if it could be fixed for the return journey. On removing the clutch cover the problem was easily spotted, the rivets on the Cosa clutch basket had disintegrated, a whole new unit was needed, and the old rivets accounted for so that they did not cause any further problems inside the engine. What was more shocking for the mechanic was not the state of the clutch, but the amount of road crud caked onto the engine and under the floorboards. I have never been someone who religiously cleans his scooter every weekend, I would rather ride it, and I don't think the scooters he was used to fixing got as much use throughout the year as mine did maybe? Thankfully the repair was completed, I paid the bill and was able to enjoy the rest of the weekend riding around the island and then the journey home to Cambridge.

This scooter served me well for a good five years, ferrying the kids around and taking me to work and back, as well as the usual rallies and ride outs of the time. It wasn't a massively powerful engine being just a standard 200cc with a Sito Plus exhaust, but it was sound and could be made to shift along at a decent pace. For the time I had it, my journey to work took me along mostly small country roads and some really fun sections with good combinations of bends, straights and a couple of hills, not that there's many of them in the area of Cambridgeshire that I lived. With the right positioning, timing and acceleration, cars could be overtaken and despatched with ease while they trundled around the bends, and I could carry on scratching along the lanes.

CRASH

One bright morning in late summer, I was heading to work along the A14 and pulled off at the Cambridge services exit to follow the usual route to work. As I rode along the first stretch of country lane, I was psyching myself up for the ride. Throttle wide open through each gear, I built up some speed for a series of bends before the village. They were all maybe 70 to 80 degree turns, and I positioned myself over towards the central road markings. The trees along the left side of the road came to an end and the view opened up, I moved the scooter further to the right to get the best line through the bend and then kept to the left, ready to swap the lean immediately over to the opposite side for the next tight right hander. As I shifted my bodyweight over to the right of the seat, letting my leg go with gravity towards the inner radius of the curve, I put some pressure through the right handlebar to tip the scooter over a touch more and twisted the throttle grip to accelerate out of the bend. My position was good to drift left onto the short straight, the power was feeding through the rear tyre onto the tarmac, and then… SHIT! I'm caught out, I hadn't anticipated what was coming next and I should have done. Leaning the scooter well over to the right, there was not much daylight between the engine casing and the road, and in that split second, I tried to keep my shoulders relaxed to stop myself steering the scooter straight and riding into the grass verge. What I see up ahead is large patch of moisture on the road in the shade of some trees which have blocked the early morning sun and stopped the road being dried out by its rays. There was nothing I could do but hope I got away with it and the tyres kept gripping the road surface. But no, my rear wheel slides to the left, the scooter lowsides and I drop onto the tarmac rolling over, two, three, four times in the road. As I come to a stop, I quickly stand up to move myself out of the danger of the two oncoming cars, only to watch the first drive by oblivious or uncomprehending of what had just happened. The second driver is thankfully more alert and pulls over to help.

I look around for my scooter, but it is nowhere to be seen. My brain catches up and tries to work out what has happened, then I spot it lying in a ditch, side panels scraped, mudguard squashed, and handlebar broken. With the help of the driver, I scramble into the ditch and we both drag the scooter out, up onto the grass bank and back onto the road to make sense of the damage. I thank the driver and, reassured that I am okay, he continues on his way as I call into work. The scooter is a write-off and once everything is settled, I see an opportunity to get back riding a Lambretta, not all things that go wrong are bad.

Bugger! Just pulled out of a ditch

TOMORROW'S DREAM

The hunt was on for another scooter. I'd had another full-bodied GP in mind for some time and would often while away time looking at available options on the internet, knowing that I wouldn't be able to justify a second scooter. Now though, there was an insurance claim in process, and I could enjoy looking for the replacement of the Vespa. Again, I scoured all the usual places looking for the right scooter. Eventually, a likely looking machine appeared in the For Sale section on the Lambretta Club of Great Britain's (LCGB) forum. Located on the far side of the Humber Bridge, it was a reasonable distance to travel if it was the right one. Originally built in India in 1986, it had recently been imported into the UK and bought by someone with the intention of cutting the bodywork down. Thankfully though, it was felt that the bodywork was too good to attack with a hacksaw and angle grinder and so it kept its panels and was spray painted in one main colour, an unusual grey/green mix that suited the model, with white used as a contrasting colour under the side panels and silver on the wheels and forks. It had previously been fitted with a tuned Imola kitted engine, but that had been removed for the sale and replaced with its original 150cc engine. I liked the scooter, it had potential and looked like it had been put together well using a hydraulic front disc brake, tubeless wheel rims, an Ancillotti Slope back sports seat, a small sprint rack and a spare wheel with a vinyl cover mounted behind the legshields. It had the look of a scooterboy machine and was enough of a blank canvas that I could stamp my identity on it over time.

Contact was made with the seller and a visit arranged to check the machine over. I drove up soon after, with a trailer attached to the car and an envelope stuffed with the cash needed in my jacket pocket. The scooter looked as it did in the pictures, and fitted the description given. The seller was very upfront about the engine, it was crap, but a good base to build something with. A test ride backed up his description, but the asking price reflected that, and I was happy to hand over the asking price, load up the trailer and head home.

Arriving home, everyone was interested to see what I had returned with, even if they didn't share the same level of enthusiasm, the kids helped me to unload the scooter and wheel it round to the shed where they left me to fawn over my new acquisition. The plan was to keep the engine as it was for a while then revamp it in the near future but riding it along the busy A14 to work over the next couple of days, it was obvious that it needed immediate attention and a little bit more oomph to cope with the traffic that I would regularly ride it in. A visit to my mate Viv at his workshop, when he traded under the banner Reaper Tuning, resulted in dropping the engine off with him for a full rebuild including new seals and bearings, a barrel rebore up to 175cc and a new piston, all mated with the carburettor and Clubman exhaust it had arrived with. Nothing flash, but affordable, reliable and a more powerful than it was when I bought it.

WHEN YOU'RE LIVING ON...

With Viv's help to validate or dismiss my ideas, this Lambretta has evolved over the years. Sometimes it was due to something breaking, like when the original standard Dellorto carburettor developed a crack on the manifold mount, and then replaced with a more up to date or effective part or as with other times, when I discovered a new piece of kit and felt it just had to have a place on my scooter. The defective carb was replaced by a 26mm Dellorto PHBH which would later lose out to a 30mm version. The Clubman exhaust rattled itself to pieces one day and sounded like a Lancaster bomber coming into land, so that was replaced with an Ancillotti Clubman that made way for a BGM V2 that improved how the engine worked but would rattle the internal baffles lose over time. I tried an expansion pipe but that didn't suit the engine so sold that on, and returned to a BGM, a V3 then a V4 both with imperfections but still effective exhausts. A big gripe I have with a lot of exhausts is the downpipe rusting away due to them often being constructed from mild steel, the high temperatures they are subjected to and road salt in the winter months. This makes them look scabby and difficult to remove from the main body or manifold, a right royal pain. Other parts that I would change or experiment with, sometimes for better sometimes for worse, were the stator plate from the original to a BGM version which, despite some riders' experiences, I always found had quite a good lifespan. Then there was the Agusto Auto Retard box, a good bit of kit that automatically moves the ignition timing through the rev range, helping to make a more efficient and reliable engine. I used one for some time but then moved away from them in a bid to simplify the set-up, particularly for when away on a trip, and thinking that as the engine wasn't actually that high revving (where the Agusto really excels) that it was a touch of overkill. The seat was swapped numerous times for both looks and, as I got older comfort, being supplemented with an Airhawk seat pad to make high mileage bearable (highly recommended). Tyres were swapped as better handling ones were made available, the wheel rims were replaced with SIP tubeless rims for safety (and because they looked really cool too!) and suspension units were swapped for more modern replacements. The list is endless and could probably fill a whole chapter by itself, but the constant thinking of how to evolve and improve my scooter for me and the riding I do, is a huge part of the fun even if not all the changes resulted in improvement, lost me money or caused frustration along the way. So much of what I know about how my scooter works and how to fix it when it doesn't, comes from changing things, experimenting, breaking it and evolving it, along with clocking the miles up riding it around, the road being the best place to find out if new parts are up to the job or not.

After a while, and to make the scooter fully my own, I decided to come up with a name for it that would adorn the side panels in the way that many scooters were decorated in the 1980s. I ruminated for some time over what to call it, whatever that name was it needed to have a meaningful connection for me. A lifelong love of music provided innumerable song titles that could potentially be used so I set about looking for one that would work. Some years ago, I would often notice a singer being mentioned in Mojo music magazine. This musician was highly regarded for both his song writing and guitar playing but he only had a short life and career. He was also held in high regard by fellow musicians, a sure sign of talent and ability. That person was Nick Drake, someone who released only three LPs in the early 1970s, and who Paul Weller cited as an influence on his Wild Wood album. I felt I needed to check out his back catalogue. When I did, I discovered music that involved highly technical but warm guitar playing and gently pastoral songs full of deep, but sometimes troubled feelings. My wife used to refer to it as suicide music, which I didn't agree with at all. To me it was beautiful, gentle music that could take you to other easier places. A few years later another musician that I discovered was John Martyn, again a highly respected and incredibly talented musician who wrote, among many fantastic pieces of work, one song about a close friend who he watched struggle through life with poor mental health. That friend happened to be Nick Drake, who died much earlier than he should have, missing the later recognition that his music deserved. Everything fitted, a musical connection with people that I revered and through Paul Weller, could link back to my first involvement with scooters. It was not the typical music that would normally be heard on rallies, which in itself appealed to me, and I could picture the title adorning the side panels of a Lambretta, my Lambretta, which was now known as Solid Air.

MONEY, THAT'S WHAT I WANT

In early 2017, Solid Air had been given a bit of a makeover with some fresh paint and an engine update using a Gran Turismo small block GT186 kit. In that setup it was put through its paces for the rest of that year and the next. These are robust and capable little kits with mine clocking up thousands of miles over those two years. However, I felt the need for a change and an engine with some extra power, but I didn't want something that needed major tuning to achieve that. I wasn't after a high revving engine either but something that would work within a reasonable rev range, which wouldn't put undue stress on the engine and its components and would hopefully be economical and fun to ride. I realise that economical and fun aren't often found in the same package, but I have a curious mind so had one eye open for an engine that might fit the bill.

Later that year, a soon to be released cylinder kit grabbed my attention. The main cylinder was cast in aluminium and incorporated the reed housing, which was a new idea. To aid cooling the cylinder fins were shaped to have extra surface area on one side helping to dissipate that heat, which along with air leaks, is an enemy of a two-stroke engine. In a similar way, the cylinder head had extra cooling fins and the piston was shaped to take heat expansion into consideration. The thinking behind the design was brilliant and really caught my imagination. To top that though, and because of the design not featuring a spigot (an extension of the cylinder bore that holds the piston in place as it moves up and down), the engine capacity was bigger than normal for the small block engine casing that Solid Air used. The kit was a whopping 210cc (huge for a small block engine) and was billed as a fast tourer with peak power around 25bhp at a relatively low 6,000 revs with a smooth and usable power delivery, right up my street. My GT kit put out about 14bhp so the extra 10bhp was significant. The new kit was known by the moniker M210Tv and made by Quattrini. I was interested and needed to know more.

The kit was generating a lot of interest in the scooter media and on the LCGB forum "Raveydavey" (aka Dave Loveday) was sharing his experience with his newly built engine and which only tempted me more, so I set about gathering the parts to build a Quattrini engine for Solid Air in the summer and the engine was built, fitted and dyno'd just before Christmas of 2018. When something new appears on the market the people who buy the product early in its life always end up being something of a guinea pig, finding out any glitches by using it in the real world and often at their own expense if things go wrong, and this was certainly the case with my Quattrini. Dave Loveday, Iggy Grainger (of SLUK) and myself all suffered engine seizures very early in our engine's lives. I had put my engine together under Viv's watchful eye and rebuilt the repaired engine, whilst the other two were repaired by the dealer that built their engines. There are too many variables to be able to accurately decide whether there was a common denominator to connect all three failures, such as riding style at the time, fuel quality, how well the engine was put together and variation in parts used (I have my theory), but all three engines were soon repaired and put back on the road. Sadly, the problems with my engine were not an easy fix and I would be troubled with numerous exhaust breakages, heat seizures and piston failures over a period of time.

The Quattrini, newly built and full of promise

FLYING 8 BALLS 2019

A small club rally, camping in a field with basic amenities and a good supply of alcoholic beverages to lubricate the tonsils, can be a joy to attend. What can beat a trip on a scooter to meet like-minded individuals and get merrily drunk while talking bollocks?

My riding partner for the weekend was Andrew Scott and we were both looking forward to the Flying 8 Balls SC rally, which was to be held at the Angel Inn at Larling in Norfolk. But as with the best laid plans, ours were severely scuppered the night before we were due to leave when Solid Air suffered yet another breakdown in what was becoming quite a saga with the Quattrini engine. On the way home from work, my scooter suffered a heat seizure while being ridden at about 70mph. Luckily it was just a case of clutch in, cruise to a stop on the hard shoulder while cursing loudly. Thankfully Andrew very kindly provided a recovery service home (or rather I called him and begged for help). Later that night with plan A having been scuppered, plans B, C and D were discussed for the weekend. Plan B involved driving the car up to the Angel Inn but bought a resounding NO from both parties. Plan C was me riding his Mugello equipped GP while he rode his daughter's Vespa 50cc auto. That was a promising idea but later in the evening Plan D emerged amid a flurry of late-night messages.

> Me: *Scotty, what about you riding your Fizzy, (a fine example of the legendary Yamaha FS1-E moped with its newly rebuilt zero miles engine) and I ride Lucy's Vespa moped?*
>
> Andrew: *Another possibility hadn't thought of that!! Are You serious?*
>
> Me: *Yes! Why not?*
>
> Me: *I would feel bad riding your GP and you riding the Vespa because I've broken my scooter.*
>
> Me: *Then we'll be equally powered! Full on ironic, everyone will love the Fizzy, and we will have at least ridden to the rally on two wheels, not four.*
>
> Andrew: *Could be a Vespa/Fizzy combo then! Speak in the morning.*

Followed in the morning by...

Andrew: *Are you sure about riding the Fizzy and Vespa?*

Me: *Yes deffo!*

As soon as the insurance company was open, Andrew made a phone call to put me onto the policy for the moped and my wife provided a taxi over to Andrew's house for a mid-morning departure. The machines are loaded, starting orders are given and with the sound of laughter and Steppenwolf's "Born to be Wild" booming inside my crash helmet we are off, whilst trying to remember that there's no foot brake pedal and the clutch lever is not a clutch lever but the rear brake! Cambridge to Larling is only about 50 miles away and a 60 minute ride normally, so with that and the low speeds of our machines we decided to take the scenic route and avoid the usual dual carriageway route of the A14 and A11, but after an hour we had only travelled the short distance to Newmarket (The land of horses and little people) and a much needed break.

What followed was a gentle and relaxing ride through the tiny winding lanes of Suffolk and Norfolk with all the time in the world to watch the roadside flowers grow while the birds squawked at us to get out of their way as we dawdled along. Our leisurely jaunt was only disrupted by a short stretch of the A134 where we really noticed our lack of top speed and the eagerness of car drivers to overtake the two moped marauders. We eventually rolled into Larling at a sedate pace in the early afternoon where our arrival was met by quizzical, and questioning looks as we arrive on the mopeds and set up our tents on the campsite. Scooterists can be a fickle bunch, people were gawping at me in dismay, despite riding what was technically a scooter, while Andrew was surrounded by middle aged men admiring his ride and recalling their own hazy days of moped riding as miscreant 16-year-olds. Good-humoured comments were made by friends regarding our chosen transport, which were taken in the spirit they were intended, and we were happy to have at least turned up on two wheels. One friend asked

Feeling the power, with Andrew Scott

whether the engine was actually running as it was so quiet. He couldn't resist unleashing the beast with a twist of throttle as I was sat on it, before remembering that it was an automatic engine, and I would have landed on my arse clutching a then empty mug of tea if he did! The afternoon was spent bumping into friends, making new ones and drinking some tasty beer in the sun before getting changed out of our riding gear to continue in the same manner for the rest of the evening.

As is often the case at any scooter rally, large or small, a good amount of alcohol was consumed, and the conversation was lively, becoming increasingly bizarre the later into the evening we got, before retreating to our tents to recover for the ride home. Bacon rolls at the Flying 8 Balls club grill and bright sunshine welcomed the new day before a predictably leisurely ride home. Andrew had to contain his excitement when we passed a seemingly endless line of oncoming supercars on a quiet country lane whilst I accidently gazed down at my petrol gauge (not realising until then that I had one) and decided we'd better find some petrol soon, despite me thinking we would get there and back on a tankful. We rode along until the FS1E suffered the

In for a penny...

only mechanical trouble of the weekend, a fouled spark plug. Not normally a problem but due to the late change of transport, no plugs had been packed, bugger! No worries we thought, I'll leave Andrew there and just quickly nip back the short distance to Thetford and find a Halfords store. Sadly though, it's not possible to "quickly nip" anywhere on a moped loaded with a 16 stone scooterboy and camping gear. Finally, over an hour later I proudly present Scotty with two of NGK's finest BR7HS spark plugs, and we continued our homeward journey towards the (thankfully) flat lands of Cambridgeshire.

THE NOT SO MAGNIFICENT SEVEN

My time with the Quattrini was tumultuous to say the least. In total, I needed to buy seven new pistons due to heat seizures and complete piston failures, when disintegration left just the crown of the piston attached to the connecting rod of the crank. I used three different exhausts in total, two of which cracked multiple times and needed welding to make them usable again, while different ignition advance/retard systems were experimented with to try and make the engine more robust. Any excessive heat issue is only going to be resolved when the cause is identified and corrected, and this is what we needed to find. Sitting in Viv's workshop one night, with us both trying to work out why the latest piston had failed (#4 piston if I am correct), Viv disappeared with the cylinder head and the words "back in a minute". On his return he placed the head on the desk and declared "That'll be the problem!" He had measured the volume of the bowl that is the combustion chamber and found it to be too small, making the compression ratio too high. This area, in the cylinder head above the piston, is where combustion takes place igniting the fuel that powers the engine. In its current state, there was not enough space in the combustion chamber in relation to the amount of fuel and air, on the compression stroke. This creates a high compression ratio, potentially producing excessive heat, our very problem. To fix this, the bowl needed to be enlarged, reducing the compression ratio and in turn, helping to reduce heat buildup which would make the engine less prone to heat seizures and therefore more reliable.

The remains of one Quattrini piston

The second issue of piston disintegration was more difficult to fix and, like the heat seize issue, not something that all Quattrini owners suffered with. The advantage of the spigot-less design of the barrel is that it allowed the capacity of the engine to be increased (meaning more power), but having a spigot provides support to the piston as there is less scope for side to side

Another part of the broken piston jigsaw

movement during its travel. Here, I feel I should say that I am not claiming to possess anywhere near the expertise or knowledge of the kit's designer, I can only report my findings through my experiences gained riding the miles I do on the type of journey that I do, then thinking about what had gone wrong and researching the subject by talking to knowledgeable people and looking at online resources.

Why one person's engine would suffer this problem and not another was baffling. The engine had been correctly set up and the crank ran true, giving the piston an easy run on its many thousands of revolutions, so we came to the possible conclusion that it might just be down to different riding styles or the amount of use? Riding a scooter very gently is going to give the engine a far easier time than one which is ridden faster, more extremely, or more often over longer more arduous journeys, and this is where we felt the difference may lie. When the piston is at the lowest point of its travel with this kit, it is not supported by a spigot and having a relatively short distance between the gudgeon pin (it's pivot point) and the top of the piston (its crown), means that the piston is not supported sufficiently at that point within the bore, allowing unwanted lateral movement which if excessive will put undue strain on the piston, causing failure. That's my experience and my diagnosis for my engine.

THE CRACK

Solid Air, my battle-scarred work horse of a scooter, is my main form of transport whatever the time of year. It carries me to work as well as around Britain and Europe to events like the LCGB Coast to Coast and Euro Lambretta rallies, meeting up with friends and escaping the rigours of everyday life along the way. Sometimes it even gets me home too!

For a few weeks it had sat forlornly on the workbench, engine out, waiting for the newly relined barrel to return, so that I could fit another new, and not so cheap, piston into it. The barrel arrived and the rebuild got underway. I had been on the spanners working on the scooter all day, I was cold, tired and hungry, my back ached and my hands were yet again engrained with oil, grease, and road muck from the engine. I was nearly done, just a couple of cables to adjust and some fastenings to tighten before I could kickstart the engine back into life. Peering under the floorboards to get a better look at the job in hand, I see something and reach for a torch to get a better look.

Fuck!

I could not believe it.

The frame had a crack running 180° from left to right, just under where the bridge piece sits. This is a major repair meaning more weeks off the road. I had been pushed to the limit leading up to this, trying to keep this bloody machine on the road and this shoved me about as close to the edge as I could get without falling off headfirst.

I cursed again and threw something forcefully into a corner before locking up, heading back indoors, and grabbing a beer.

A fix was needed. I called Viv to explain what I had found, and with him a plan was made. After stripping the frame of all its bodywork and components, I drove it up to his workshop near Darlington. Viv intended to cut through the frame where the crack was, insert a metal spigot into one half of the frame tube before pushing the other half onto the spigot. This would rejoin the two pieces of the frame and a seam of weld would secure the two sections together, in theory. This approach did not go quite to plan. When he tried to fit the spigot, it forced the frame tube to splay outwards weakening the area around the join and halting the repair. Over the phone he explained the situation to me. There were two choices, find a replacement frame or fix it as well as possible using the original plan and then strengthen the frame with more metalwork. Weighing everything up, I eventually decided that keeping the original frame and reinforcing it with some metal plate welded around the frame would achieve what was needed. Solid Air may end up a millimetre or two shorter and a touch heavier, but it would be fixed, rebuilt and soon be back on the road where it belonged.

THE BULLDOG RUN 2021

In the June of 2021, with the frame recently repaired the barrel lining and piston were gently run in on the way down to the west country for a day's riding, that Andy Neville had organised for members of Bristol Lambretta Club (BLC) and a few other local clubs. We spent the day riding around Bristol and Somerset and stopped overnight to sample some delightful local ciders at a pub with a campsite conveniently attached to it. The trip was successfully completed and a few weeks later I headed north to meet Nigel Sleightholm and ride over to Berwick-upon-Tweed for the Berwick SC Bulldog Run. These two trips were welcome relief following the tedium of the countrywide lockdown and the worldwide COVID-19 pandemic at the time.

Bob Darling, of the Berwick Bulldogs SC, deserved a big well done for staging this event during a world pandemic. Organising any scooter related event is difficult enough in normal times, and hats off to those people too, but poor old Bob, who had already had three earlier dates postponed persevered to finally stage their Bulldog Run in 2021. I first met Bob in 2019

A photo opportunity in the Trough of Bowland, Lancashire

at the LCGB Derby 150 and having previously taken part, Nigel Sleightholm and Paul Thomson recommended that I travel north for a weekend of riding some fantastic roads around the Scottish border. Two years later, Nigel and I were thoroughly looking forward to the trip which somehow coincided with a weather forecast of blazing sunshine. Sadly, Paul couldn't join us as he was recovering from knee replacement surgery, the curse of the middle-aged scooterboy.

Berwick-upon-Tweed, home understandably of the Berwick Bulldogs SC, was the base for the weekend. I have never had the chance to visit the town before and was very pleasantly surprised. It's a beautiful place, steeped in history which includes many changes of power between the English and Scottish and which is still a bone of contention among some of the scooter riding locals it seems, if only in jest(?). One piece of advice though, if you do visit Berwick take a hat. The town is "decorated" by the local seagull population, and it is not unusual to see a parked car that looks like a very slap-dash decorator has been working nearby and forgot to use any dust sheets. Keep a beady eye looking upwards at all times, the local Herring gulls are not at all fussy as to where to drop their load, as I was to find out.

The message was put out that the local Wetherspoons would be the hub for Friday night and so drinks were drunk, chat was had, and the mickey was taken by those present at The Leaping Salmon. While we were sat at a table outside, as per COVID-19 rules and following the orders of the slight but fiery waitress, the peace was shattered when an incoming gull scored a bullseye on our table with its fishy missile, and I suffered as a casualty from a ricochet of gull shit that struck me right in the eye, providing endless laughs for those sat around me! Apparently, it's lucky but I'm not so sure. Don't say I didn't warn you.

The following morning all the scooters taking part in the run gathered on the quayside before making their way northwards out of town. Very soon we are into tiny country lanes which opened out into some lovely smooth and sweeping bends leading to the harbour at St Abbs, a beautiful spot with crystal clear water and loads of people out enjoying the sun, their newfound freedom and the attraction of our scooters turning up en masse. I heard one of the locals say to his mate as we left, "Wow that smell of two-stroke, don't it take you back!" Bob had obviously put a lot of effort into planning the route which gave us a good mix of roads to ride. There was plenty to keep us on our toes too, whether it was tractors filling up the tiny lanes, gravel just where you didn't want it, stunningly beautiful scenery with castles and views that suddenly appeared when you crested the brow of a hill, along with wild and open moors where you could see all the way to Edinburgh and the Firth of Forth and bizarre sights like a monk in full habit wandering the lanes, seemingly in the middle of nowhere. The riding was fantastic, Solid Air's Quattrini engine was running sweetly, particularly when the moors opened up and I could make use of the whole road, winding the throttle open and connecting all the bendy bits up, pure and simple scooter riding joy.

The day left everyone satisfyingly exhausted, but Nigel and I still had the energy to find a kebab shop before wandering up to the evening's meeting place for drinks and laughs, of which there was plenty. Again, everyone was very friendly and welcoming, but we did exchange unsure glances when towards the end of the night the previous 500 hundred years of Anglo-Scottish relations were heatedly discussed with raised voices. Thankfully all the taunts were in good humour, and this was confirmed with the odd sly grin or subtle wink in our direction. Sunday and the long ride home to Cambridgeshire comes all too soon. Nigel heads back to Lancaster and I head south along the scenic coastal route taking me past Holy Island and the highly impressive Bamburgh Castle before rejoining the A1.

Bob Darling of the Berwick Bulldogs SC saying hello, somewhere in Scotland

Bamburgh Castle, on the way home from the Bulldog Run

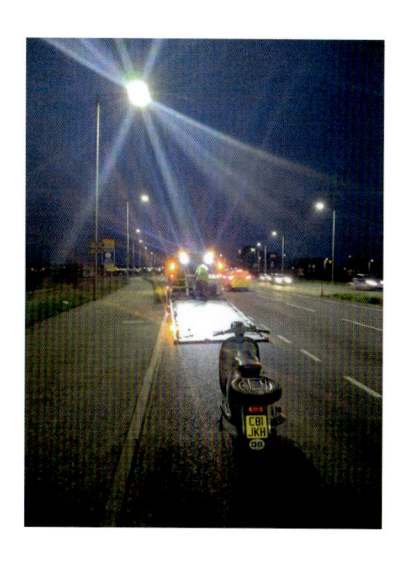

Another lift home on a breakdown recovery lorry

QUATTRINI: ITALIAN, MEANING MONEY, A SMALL ITALIAN COIN

A memorable weekend had come to an end, but the highs are all too often followed by a low. Heading home, Solid Air's Quattrini engine frustratingly suffered yet another breakdown, only four weeks and 1400 miles after having fitted a newly relined barrel and piston. Arriving home and stripping the engine down, I decided that the time had come to bring my tempestuous affair with the Quattrini to an end, however good an engine it was to ride. It had become unfeasibly and repetitively expensive. Not to worry though, thinking cap on, I was sure there would be a solution and a replacement engine just waiting to be built.

Every time my Quattrini engine suffered a breakdown, my wallet was hit and hit hard, along with the inconvenience of my scooter, and main transport, being forced out of use. At the time, a new piston would cost between £150 and £180 with a relining of the barrel surface also being needed due to the associated damage, which would cost over £150. This was not economically sustainable for long. There is a point to which it is acceptable to go, to keep ploughing hard earned money into a project when it is felt that the result is worthwhile, and then there is another point at which defeat must be accepted and I had finally reached that point. The Quattrini engine was removed from Solid Air and disgracefully retired.

BACK TO BASICS

I needed dependability from the scooter engine that took me to work on a daily basis, let alone to LCGB Events at home and Euro rallies abroad. Talking with Viv about options and having sold the GT186 kit to fund the Quattrini build, it was decided that I would return to a cast iron barrel matched with a Suzuki TS piston, Dellorto PHBH carburettor and Clubman exhaust using the current small block engine casing. This would be a good balance of being relatively cheap to put together using parts I already had and providing enough power to get me where I wanted to go and in a reasonable amount of time. The engine did everything that was required of it, if in a slower, less exciting way than how the Quattrini would have done it, but it did it every day without complaint, what more can I ask for? What more? Well, more power if I am honest. I missed the ability to overtake pretty much any car whenever I wanted to, quickly and safely, and I missed having an engine that could easily reach the national speed limit and hold it, barring the strongest of winds that would make me reduce my speed anyway, it being too uncomfortable to ride at that speed while being buffeted around in the saddle. Then one day I had a brainwave. The Quattrini Barrel was sitting on the shelf gathering dust and the only use I could think of for it was as a doorstop. I did not like being defeated by it, so putting together a couple of recent but separate conversations, I realised there may be a way. All that was needed to make my Quattrini engine work consistently and reliably, was to somehow incorporate a spigot into the barrel to provide support for the piston at the bottom of its travel.

It was not a new idea to fit an aluminium barrel with a cast iron sleeve, but I wondered if it would work with the Quattrini Barrel? Rather than stop at the base of the barrel, could we continue it further to make a spigot? Viv was tasked with dry building the top end and taking some measurements to see if a piston could be found that would fit the job. Having a cast iron bore would also be cheaper to repair than a nikasil lined barrel and I would be more likely to be able to continue a journey if the engine suffered a mild heat seize. When damaged an iron bore can be more forgiving compared a nikasil one, as had happened previously travelling to the LCGB Isle of Mull rally.

Viv worked out that the idea was doable and that a Yamaha 350 piston would fit the role. With that good news, the barrel was sleeved, and a piston purchased and matched. Sharing this on a Quattrini Owners Facebook page, I found out that someone else had also successfully done this to a damaged barrel for a sprint scooter, so confidence was high that we were onto something. After what felt like a prolonged wait, but actually wasn't, the sleeved barrel was returned, and the engine was rebuilt. A dyno session gave a good impression of the new setup and I got to work putting some miles on the clock to run it in.

Writing this now in 2023, my "semi skimmed" 190cc Quattrini engine has been in use for 18 months. In that time, it has been pushed hard and only suffered one complication with the piston rings after about 3 months. The first piston we used was from a RD350, that seemed to wear its rings past an acceptable tolerance limit after 3-4,000 miles. The result of this was one of the ring pegs came lose, allowing the ring to move and get chewed up in between the piston and the barrel wall. To get round this, the second piston came from a RZ350, the ring ends for this piston were a slightly different design which Viv felt would not cause the same problem with wear for the ring peg. Many miles later, including five endurance races, the Euro rally in Belgium, the LCGB Coast to Coast twice, a 3,000+ mile Scandinavian trip and numerous trips north up to Darlington, where Viv is based, commuting all year round as well as just riding the scooter for the sheer hell of it, Solid Air is still on the same RZ piston and the sleeved down conversion has proved its worth, backing up my view that the barrel spigot provides the support that the piston needs with this kit.

The 210cc Quattrini kit for the Lambretta is without doubt, an amazing bit of kit using modern motorcycle technology and, when it wasn't breaking pistons, was a wonderful engine to ride. It has the added bonus of being within reach of normal scooter riders (if there is such a thing?) without being engine exotica and needing the bank balance of a small principality to buy. The engine can be raced, rallied, or commuted on with ease. It is a pleasure to ride gently but twist the throttle back in anger and the scooter is off up the road like a scalded cat, providing the rider with a lot of grin inducing fun! There are many people riding Quattrini equipped Lambrettas that have not experienced the same problems as I have, and I am pleased for them, but I should have had shares in the piston company with the quantity I bought over the four years of running the kit. I wrote about my problems with the kit on the LCGB forum and social media to share my experiences and to help people if they were having the same issues. The whole experience was great fun if frustrating at times and I learnt a hell of a lot from it, but it did cost me a lot of money with all the problems I met along the way. In the end I proved, to myself at least, that being able to build an engine was not the issue. I do feel that hard riding (not a lack of mechanical sympathy) along with high mileage can put extra strain on the piston because of the kits design, leading to failure, and that for me, incorporating a spigot into the barrel makes a great kit more robust with it than without.

TRIGGER'S SIX MILLION DOLLAR BROOM

The combined joys and frustrations of owning a classic vehicle of any sort are innumerable, from the satisfaction of travelling in a vehicle that should have probably been scrapped years earlier, to the pride that is felt when someone admires the object of your valuable time and hard-earned money. But the frustration experienced when yet again, a part fails, or a breakdown threatens an upcoming trip, can test even the strongest person's character.

In the BBC comedy series Only Fools and Horses, the character Trigger produces a photograph of his faithful road sweeping broom to prove that it is the same item he had used for the past twenty years, amid consternation from Del Boy, Rodney and Boycie. Trigger then confuses the issue by stating in his typical droll way, "Mind you, the Broom has had 17 new heads and 14 new handles".

In another television series from my childhood, The Bionic Man, after the main character Steve Austin suffered catastrophic injuries, it was claimed that "We can rebuild him... better than he was before. Better, stronger, faster." It was becoming clearer to me the longer I owned Solid Air, that Trigger's Six Million Dollar Broom would be a very apt addition to its title. Six million dollars because it feels like I must have spent close to that amount keeping the bloody thing running, and Triggers Broom because so many parts had been or will have been replaced at some point in its life. But if it breaks, I will rebuild it!

Some of my enamel badges collected since the 1980s

126

PART 3

GROWN UP RALLIES...

Lambretta Club Great Britain

In the 1980s I knew of the LCGB but felt it was probably more for the serious, grown up scooterist, people who had been riding for years, maybe raced and knew their way round a Lambretta engine blindfolded, whilst I was just a young upstart new to the scene with no real knowledge of the Lambretta, its history and how to keep one running reliably. I would occasionally pick up a copy of the club magazine Jetset from somewhere, and read of club rallies on a much smaller scale than the Nationals that I attended, and read of AGMs, club news and rallies on a much smaller scale than the Nationals that I attended, and get to recognise the names of club stalwarts such as Kev Walsh, John Law and Mike Karslake. The thing that made a mark on me back then, was that the riding of the scooters was as important as owning them. A lot of the events were not about riding scooters there, parking them up for the weekend and then spending the rest of the weekend in the pub, but about riding them as part of the weekend, whether it was over a scooter assault course or riding around the countryside before settling down in a nice pub and catching up with other members over a few beers. I read about events such as the club rally at Tan Hill, the opening of Mike Karslake's Lambretta museum and the first Euro Lambretta Jamboree in 1989. Seeds were planted in my mind and many years later I would find myself taking part in similar LCGB events.

I finally joined the LCGB when I rebuilt my cutdown, just as computers and the internet were becoming more accessible and a much bigger part of everyone's life. Via the world wide web, I discovered scooter related forums such as Scooterboy World, Scooterotica and of course the LCGB members forum. These virtual places are frequented by people with a wealth of knowledge about both Vespas and Lambrettas that they are prepared to share online with others, and a place where conversations could be had, and friendships started with like-minded people who could often be met at scooter events and rallies. I have met many people because of the LCGB forum, benefited from tips and advice and shared my exploits with Solid Air with other forum users, and without wanting to sound too corny, my scootering life has been richer because of it.

THE COAST TO COAST

I had known about the Coast to Coast (C2C) for some time. This long distance walk of nearly 190 miles was made famous by Arthur Wainwright, an accountant who found solace as a fell walker and wrote a series of beautifully written and illustrated books describing his walks. Starting in St Bees on the Cumbrian coast, the walk follows cross country footpaths taking you through stunning national parks and unspoilt countryside until the destination of Robin Hoods Bay on the east coast of North Yorkshire is reached. The tradition is that you dip your booted feet into the sea at either end. It is something that would make a great adventure and test anyone's personal endurance, one day I might even do it.

The other way to take this challenge is on a Lambretta scooter in the company of a load of other scooter riding enthusiasts that may not want to dip their boots in the sea but who would be very happy to sample some other more thirst satisfying liquids in a pub at either end of the ride. The LCGB had been running this event for some years and I got to know of it through the forum and the club magazine. Having it on my own personal radar of things to do for a while, I took part in my first LCGB C2C in 2015 with Andrew Scott, and ever since it has been one of my favourite events on the calendar.

My first LCGB Coast to Coast, with Andrew Scott in 2015

Andrew Scott taking in the view from Wrynose Pass

LCGB scooter legshield banners

131

Taking In The View
Hardknott ideas.

signs & phone box view

SOLIDAIR

HARDKNOTT

caution signs?

HARKNOTT

Scooter with Romans chasing?

Text

OS map?

Lakeland Sheep?

ROMAN FORT

Built by the Romans around 110AD.
33%
300m
1.2 miles

HARDKNOTT

A series of unnerving hairpin bends, the Hardknott Pass is one of the steepest and most challenging roads in Britain.

Built by the Romans around 110AD, it is a single track road between Eskdale and Duddon Valley. Connecting with Wrynose Pass it is 1.2 miles long, has gradients up to 33% and a total ascent of 300 metres. It is often closed in the winter due to ice making it too treacherous to drive..... Good luck!

The route is different each time and the direction, east to west or west to east, and is regularly changed to keep the event fresh. Whether it is St Bees or Grange-over-Sands in the west to Saltburn or Bridlington in the east, the ride in between will be varied and at times challenging. The route might take you across desolate moors, along single-track roads with steep inclines or through military firing ranges, and there is no doubt that this event is about the riding. If you fancy riding the same roads that the Tour de France used in 2014, such as the spectacular Buttertubs pass with its steep inclines, enjoy stunning scenery like that found in the Lake District, or you fancy pushing your ability to the limit riding places like the Hardnott (a personal favourite) or the Kirkstone passes, then the LCGB Coast to Coast is most definitely for you.

Somewhere in the North Pennines

THE DERBY 150

In 2017 the LCGB introduced a new event to its calendar. In contrast to the C2C, the Derby 150 was a circular route from the weekend's base at the Derby rugby club and generally runs on alternate years to the C2C. Being only a couple of hours ride from home meant it was a bloody good excuse to head off and spend a day riding around the beautiful Peak District. Friday afternoon would see most people arrive, set up camp in the rugby club grounds and head to the on-site bar for food, organised by the LCGB and supplied by the friendly rugby club staff. The LCGB events are small in comparison to the national rallies, the atmosphere is welcoming, and I've always found it friendly. Attending club events, you will see the regular faces as well as people who would just take part in occasional events. Often conversations would be struck up with someone that had been met during the days ride or having recognised from other events, such as a Euro rally, and let's face it, riding the machines that we do in the way that we do, there is always something to talk about!

The Peak District is renowned for its scenic beauty and the route organisers always endeavour to provide the most scenic and challenging route possible. Earlier events have taken us through the grounds of the stately home Chatsworth House, along tiny hedge lined lanes, through dales and across dams holding back millions of gallons of water as well as along famous roads such as the Cat and Fiddle or the Snake Pass. Like the C2C, the Derby 150 is not a race and because of the types of roads used, speed limits are low and there are plenty of signs warning of Police helicopters monitoring road users' speeds in the name of safety. These roads do attract a high volume of traffic on both two and four wheels, so progressive riding is often difficult and risks a costly speeding ticket. Despite Big Brother watching, this journey is always satisfying and is all about enjoying the ride, taking in the view, and having a chat with other riders during stop offs. I have ridden in torrential rain along twisty, downhill single-track roads where the falling rain has dragged hazardous gravel directly onto the riding line causing some heart stopping moments, and on others had to endure sweltering temperatures, which can be just as arduous. One year, riding down the Snake Pass a rider found himself suddenly much closer to the tarmac than he should have when the frame on his Series 1 Lambretta suddenly snapped and folded in on itself. He found himself fighting to keep both himself and his scooter upright using his feet as stabilisers. Luckily, he was able to bring the scooter safely to a standstill and, was recovered back to base by the LCGB support vehicle that followed along and swept up mechanical casualties. Later, the scooter stood in the car park for everyone to inspect and debate in amazement at both the riders fortune and the misfortune of the frame invisibly corroding from the inside out. When I found the crack on Solid Air's frame, it made me think straight back to this broken scooter and realise how lucky I was to have spotted the problem while the scooter was on the work bench and not on a remote and twisty country road or while being thrashed around a racetrack.

On the Derby 150

Another year the luck was with me. Heading back to the rugby club along the A6, Solid Air's exhaust suddenly became noticeably louder having fractured on the down pipe. I made enquiries at a small old fashioned petrol station whether they might know of a welder that could repair the exhaust to hopefully get me home. At around 4pm on a Saturday afternoon this was a very tall order, but amazingly just down the road an engineer was working in his unit and was prepared to attempt the fix. Whipping the exhaust off, our group couldn't believe my luck in finding this cooperative welder who gave a disclaimer of "I can't guarantee how long it will last", because of the condition of the metal he was working with, but he returned the repaired pipe in exchange for a "drink" for his time, what a star! We successfully completed the journey to the rugby club and savoured a few drinks ourselves, along with some hearty food after the ride, retelling the tale of the lucky repair to willing listeners through the evening. The welder, in his wisdom was right though. Reaching Oakham on the way home the next day, my luck ran out and the exhaust gave up the ghost, leaving me to call on breakdown recovery to get me back while my riding companions continued onwards towards their own homes. Riding a Lambretta, regardless of how much preparation has been put into the scooter, you never can guarantee completing the journey, but this is often where pub tales and long-lasting memories are made.

THE ISLE OF MULL MEMBERS RALLY 2016

During a trip up to the Isle of Mull, Solid Air suffered a couple of big problems, one of which eventually proved terminal for the weekend. Heading along the A1, Solid Air was running nicely and gave no indication of any problems until completely out of the blue, the engine slurred to a stop in the right-hand lane of the carriageway while riding at just over 60mph. I pulled the clutch in, swore and with a quick wave of my left arm, coasted over to a very conveniently placed layby. The engine was locked solid, and I was only a couple of hours from home with many miles still to go. There was nothing else for it but to strip down the top end of the engine by the side of the road to see if the problem was fixable.

Tools were unpacked and I got to work. Rear floorboards off, carburettor detached, exhaust removed, and engine dropped from the frame. I could now, with a bit of persuasion, remove the cylinder head and barrel to have a look at the piston. Removing the components told me what had happened, the metal gasket between the head and barrel had failed, causing an air leak to alter the fuel/air mix which had then caused an unwanted build-up of heat. With the extra heat produced, the piston expands and effectively welds itself (briefly if you're lucky) to the wall of the bore. Also in this case, the two piston rings, that hold it steady in the bore, were damaged and stuck in the grooves that they sit in. A moment or two of head scratching took place before I pulled out my trusty Swiss Army Knife and gently scored along the edges of the rings to free them up. To my amazement this worked so that I was able to gently prise them free, clean the groove and smooth off any scuff marks with some emery paper to then refit all the components. With this done I turned the petrol back on, pressed the thumb choke lever and crossed my fingers. Prodding the kickstart I was met with good resistance, another kick and the engine sparked into life then, with a few blips on the throttle, it settled to a steady tick over speed.

Success! I packed up my tools, got my hands as clean as I could and set off again, following the signs for A1 and the North. Good progress was made up to Scotch Corner where I left the A1 then followed the A66 for a bit before turning off the main road to ride across some wonderful countryside in the North Pennines, through Alston and then on towards Carlisle to pick up the M6 towards Scotland. From there I followed the A74(M) and then turned off towards Leadhills for a stopover at The Hopetoun Arms, where I was able to pitch my tent in the garden then enjoy a pub meal and a couple of beers before heading off in the morning.

Delayed on the way to the Isle of Mull

The stunning North Pennines near Alston, on the way to the Isle of Mull

The following morning was wet and dreary when I poked my head out of the tent so there was nothing else to be done but pack up and head towards Glasgow, working my way through the early morning traffic. Riding the road alongside Loch Lomond everything felt good, I pulled over to have a break and a mug of tea from a café at Luss but on returning to my scooter I was flummoxed by its refusal to start again. There were no worrying signs before the stop and try as I might, I had no success in getting the engine going. There was nothing for it but to call the breakdown recovery people and return south to have a quiet weekend at home.

Thinking I'd be back later that evening I messaged home to let them know and very quickly received a response from my wife… "Call me before you get picked up!" Wondering what was going on to receive such a concise message I made the call. After explaining what had happened and asking for some tea to be saved, I was told not to head home but to have a guess where she was. Having no idea what was going on I asked her where? "We're on the Isle of Mull, thought we'd come up to surprise you and spend the weekend there!" And surprise me they did. I now had to arrange for Solid Air to head home on its own with the AA and find out how to get to Oban to catch the ferry across to Mull. I was in luck, asking in the café, I found out I only needed to walk 100 yards along the road to catch a bus for a two hour ride to Oban. Isle of Mull, here I come.

A few hours later, I was giving my wife and son a surprised hug at Mull's ferry terminal before being dropped off at the venue for the weekend. Dragging all my riding and camping gear out of the back of the family car bought some perplexed looks from others that had ridden there and even though I knew I had done my best to arrive on two wheels it still felt strange. Lesley and Arthur kept themselves busy sightseeing around the island while I joined the other rally goers, chatting and explaining the trials of my journey up. The Indecipherables SC took me under their wing for a bit and Karl Claydon from Loughton kindly gave me a lift on his scooter up to Tobermory so I could at least experience some of the island's roads. It would have been too much for his scooter to lug me all the way around the rugged and hilly island, so I cadged a lift back to the campsite in the back up van belonging to one of the Indecipherables.

Despite the scooter breaking down, the weekend was a success, and as often happens as a solo rider, I met new people, enjoyed a few beers with them, and made some new friends in the form of Nigel Sleightholm, Paul Thomson, and Dave Clark, who I would get to know better in a few years' time. Solid Air arrived home a few days later and was promptly stripped down for a postmortem. The flywheel boss had fractured, preventing the electrical system from working, and so a new flywheel was ordered. It was at this point that I persuaded myself (or more importantly, my wife) that a full rebuild was needed as Solid Air was now looking rather scruffy, so over the winter the opportunity was taken to smarten the whole scooter up for a fresh start the following year.

THE EURO LAMBRETTA JAMBOREE

Way back in 1989 the first Euro Lambretta Jamboree was held at Strasbourg in France. The event was the first of many and it is still going strong some 30+ years later. Each year the rally is held in a different location with the hosting duties being taken on by that country's national Lambretta Club. Because of the distances often covered to reach the destination, many British riders make a holiday of it, taking the scenic route or stopping off at points of interest along the way. Some will ride in small groups and others as part of a big club, with a back up van to carry luggage, spares and tools making the riding lighter and easier. Camping offers a cheaper option for accommodation as well as adding to the sense of adventure, but many forgo the adventure to keep their home comforts, particularly as they get older, so book themselves into a hotel or B&B along the way. Whatever makes the trip work for the individual makes the trip work, but the British scooter riders are renowned for attending in the highest numbers of all the national clubs and for their willingness to ride long distances to attend the rally. Occasionally some will transport their scooter in a van, due to work commitments or the effect of the ravages of time and long distance riding on backs, hips, or knees, and that is all fine because as the phrase goes "it's the taking part that counts."

I didn't start attending the Euro rallies until 2016 but remember reading magazine write-ups from years before. From what I read, the earlier ones had an old-time feel, quite low key and more for the mature scooter enthusiast who was maybe concerned with accuracy and authenticity of their scooter's presentation. Through the day there might be a scooter gymkhana and games on the ridden machines in a field with hay bales and wood seesaws to negotiate, while on the Saturday evening everyone would sit down to a civilised meal and glasses of wine with their food. There would be a good number of scooterists that could also be found on at the national rallies there, and they would mix with the older generation that had been involved with Lambrettas for a very long time. The Euro Jamboree is still very much like this in its feel and ethos. It is not a raucous affair (generally), it is about the ride, the scooter and the camaraderie having ventured many miles to reach the destination. There may well still be a scooter gymkhana and even traditional music, or dancing put on by the hosts for entertainment, but there may also be a racetrack to ride your scooter around, a chance to test its sprinting ability or its power output on a rolling road. There is still a gala meal for everyone to attend on the Saturday evening, which is a feat of mass catering, and there are always promises to friends old and new to meet up at the next year's rally. The Euro Lambretta Jamboree is a great event that shows off the humble machines that we love to ride, often needing to fix them along the way to reach our goal. It proves that these machines are worthy of much more than their original given purpose and we often astound the many people we meet along the way, by what we set out to do.

GERMANY 2016

Geiselwind in Germany was my first Euro experience with Andrew Scott and David Childs, who came along for the ride. We ventured through France and Belgium into Germany, dealing with small mechanical and electrical niggles along the way, got used to driving on the wrong side of the road again and occasionally took a wrong turn, but nothing we experienced did more than challenge our brain cells in seeking a fix. Along the way we visited both the Spa-Francorchamps racetrack in Belgium and the infamous Nürburgring in Germany. We sampled and fell in love with, the delicious beers on offer, particularly at Ypres in Belgium when we stopped over and visited the Menin Gate for the very moving Last Post ceremony that remembers the fallen soldiers of the first world war.

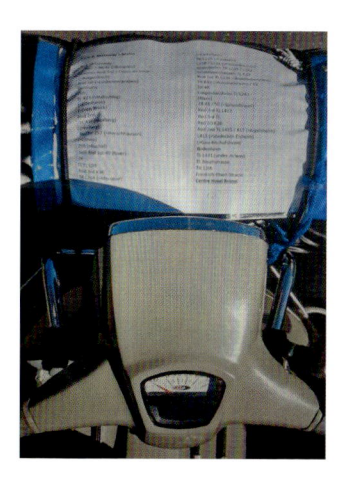

Heading home from Geiselwind

Hoping not to get lost in Germany

EURO LAMBRETTA RALLIES

LIBRAMONT-CHEVIGNY 2022

MAGNY-COURS 2024

ABEJAR 2018

	MILES
GEISELWIND:	700
ADRIA:	1100
ABEJAR:	1050
ZAKOPANE:	1250
LIBRAMONT-CHEVIGNY:	450
MAGNY-COURS IN 2024:	TBC

GEISELWIND
2016

ZAKOPANE
2019

ADRIA
2017

143

As we got closer to the event we rode through mile after mile of built up motorway traffic in searing heat and experienced the thrill and buzz of arriving safely at a scooter rally, but with a much greater sense of achievement because of the distances covered. These rallies have the same camaraderie as those held at home, with tales to tell from along the way but with a bigger variety of languages to be heard there among the rally goers. I love the Euro Rallies; they give me a reason to set out, cross the English Channel on my scooter and then head off into Europe. It is the reason for going, but the rally is only the halfway point along an adventure that needs to be embraced and experienced to be fully appreciated.

ITALY 2017

Having had my enthusiasm stoked for an annual European trip, I spent a lot of time thinking and planning for the next Jamboree at Adria in Northern Italy. Andrew and Dave couldn't join me this time, but the trip was too good to miss, and I would set off as a team of one. Riding solo abroad doesn't faze me really, having done plenty in the UK and these days, with mobile phones, satnavs and the internet with websites providing easy to book accommodation at short notice if needed, it's a lot easier than when I ventured abroad in the early 1990s. Where the scooter is concerned, preparation is the key and a good stock of tools and spares always comes in handy. I can work my way through many mechanical problems and if I cannot then my best mate Viv is only a phone call away with his expertise. European breakdown recovery will normally ensure the scooter gets back home a couple of weeks later if a breakdown is terminal, but the spares I carry will fix many problems. It's better to be carrying a good amount of gear if it makes the chances of reaching the destination higher and it would only be the mechanical equivalent of a heart transplant that would stop me trying. So, what's to lose? I could stay at home, moping around wishing I had ventured abroad, or I could head off, flying by the seat of my armoured pants, with a fully loaded scooter, a dose of good luck and a sense of adventure to see what happens along the way.

Leaving home and heading for the Eurotunnel at Folkestone, I had an easy run along the motorway but was met with the threat of a storm by some stunning cloud formations overhead as I approached the terminal. The waiting area was packed with holiday makers, bikers and fellow Adria bound scooters, who run for cover when the heavens do open, and it is always a good place to meet up with friends or get chatting to new ones.

Once in France, the plan was to avoid the motorways and see some sights. Riding along quiet curvy French country roads I would see abandoned custom's checkpoints and an impressive hilltop fort before reaching the long straight Belgian roads that go straight up and over some very big hills, quite different to what I'm used to at home. I was instructed to stop by some not very smiley police outriders for a passing bike race and received loads of hellos in the form of handlebar level two fingered victory waves or stuck out legs from European bikers. In a small German village, I nearly ran over an escaped goat with a furious German boy in pursuit which had me laughing for some miles, and I passed a massive steelworks with huge piles of crushed metal cubes, not a good place to leave the scooter unattended for too long. I rode through seemingly abandoned villages and a national park with sublimely smooth and twisty roads that took me over the River Rhein and into the Black Forest where, if you time it right, you can smell the delicious aroma of schnaps being distilled by the locals, and then I rode on to the wonderful B500 Schwarzwaldhockstrasse (Black Forest High Road).

Solid Air had a humble GT190 engine fitted at the time, which will never test this road fully with its wide sweeping curves looking down at the surrounding countryside, but it is a wonderful road with great views to soak up. I was pushing the scooter along quite progressively until, after many miles, I approach a T-Junction and shut the throttle off. What I expect to happen next doesn't. The engine revs should drop and come to a gentle idle but no, completely unexpectedly they scream like a banshee as the throttle sticks open. My heart races, I imagine shooting across the junction, crashing into a passing car with the engine revving to its limit but luckily, I am able to pull the clutch lever in and kill the engine with the ignition key just in time. It hadn't happened before that moment and didn't again after, it was just a one-off, a heart-stopping, out of the blue anomaly, thankfully!

One morning in Germany, I thought it would be a good idea to clean the air filter as it was covered in dust. I soon discovered that it is not advisable to use carb cleaner for this purpose as it dissolves the glue holding the pieces of foam together. I had to hurriedly find a local shop that could sell me a needle and thread to join the two pieces back together. It's a good job I learnt how to sew as kid. I reach the Austrian Alps where, for some time, I seem to be riding endlessly downhill and then through a long tunnel of some miles where the traffic starts to build. I approach the first traffic jam of the trip but I'm able to glide past the lot along the middle of the road. The Austrian roadworkers showed scant regard for health and safety or protective clothing going by their appearance, one being dressed in only boots, shorts, a suntan, and a cowboy hat.

Somewhere in the Austrian Alps

Near Trento in Northern Italy

The roads eventually head upwards into Italy and an immediate reduction in road surface quality, with potholes, and loose gravel everywhere. Confused by signage in the Italian campsite where I am staying, I ask why the German greeting of "guten Tag" is listed before the Italian version of Buongiorno? To be informed succinctly, "We are German here". I stopped and said hello to some Swiss Lambretta riders also bound for Adria. They were all on standard 125cc machines riding at 40 to 45mph and were impressed at my 55 to 60mph cruising speed. Riding up the side of Monte Bondone, I lost count of the hairpin bends, the road builders couldn't have squeezed in anymore. I was having great fun linking up all the twists and turns and took advantage of the long downhill gradients to coast along, saving fuel as the tank perilously neared empty and I looked for a petrol station.

I was staying at a lovely campsite on the shore of Lake Garda, somewhere I have wanted to visit for a long time. On arrival I quickly put up my tent then had a refreshing swim in the lake right in front of my pitch. Feeling revitalised, I then set off to ride the SP38 Strada della Forra, reputedly one of the most beautiful drives in the world that featured in the James Bond film Quantum of Solace. For a while I have the joy of no panniers or luggage weighing my scooter down and can fully enjoy the ride on what is a stunning road with beautiful scenery, steep climbs, severe drops, narrow tunnels, hairpin bends and small Italian villages, the whole gamut. In one village I even get an enthusiastic cheer from some locals sitting outside a bar, brilliant!

The next day I ride over Monte Bondo then onto busy and boringly straight urban roads. In Verona I hit a big lump in the road and the front luggage rack bounces off the top of the legshields. Somehow, I was able to catch it just in time and came to a stop as quickly as I could and resecured it. I made a detour into Padova to ride around the tiny, cobbled streets there, stopping for a coffee and gelato at a kiosk over looking a huge palazzo full of impressive classical statues. The kiosk owner gave me a warm and impressed welcome in incredibly good English, which he tells me he had learnt when he lived on the Tottenham Court Road in London and was fantastic company for half an hour.

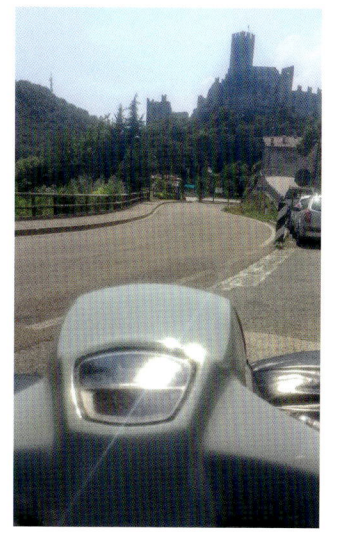

A tiny section of the beautiful SP38 Strada della Forra

Castel Drena near Lake Garda

Now the last leg to Adria. Made up of straight roads, flat fields, and drainage waterways, it's just like being back home in Cambridgeshire. An impressive welcome pack was given out on arrival, the site looked great, drinks were drunk, and I met friends old and new. Pitching my tent next to a lovely couple from Chesterfield, Donna and Richard Griffiths, I was invited over to share a beer with them, and their friends Buzz and Nick. Riding solo isn't so bad, you meet people that you wouldn't normally when in a large group and they often want to fill you up with beer and food too, which can't be bad.

There were scooters being ridden round the on-site racetrack and all the latest goodies from the dealers were on display in the main hall. Outside, the biggest BBQ I've ever seen took 24 hours to roast a whole cow! There were ride outs to join in with and a wonderful food tasting market laid on by the Lambretta Clubs of Italy who took great pride in freely handing out their local delicacies. I will never forget the delightfully fresh buffalo mozzarella cheese I was able to enjoy there, I had never tasted cheese like it before. In the company of Alan Baker and Kev from London, who I had got chatting to on the outward Eurotunnel crossing, we ate our way around Italy. Our hosts were amazing with their generous hospitality, dishing out their wares to everybody present, and sharing their well-known love of food.

Savouring some Italian culinary delights with Alan Baker

Heading into the mountains and towards Stelvio Pass

On the return journey, I had some company for a few days in the form of a "posh scooterboy" and a "veggie, anarchist-punk" from Bristol Lambretta Club, aka Ian Flynn and Andy Neville. I "met" Andy through the LCGB forum as it turned out we were riding similar routes to Adria and so we had arranged to meet up at the rally. At our first overnight stop the locals we meet love our scooters, unlike the Portuguese national flyfishing team manager, who we somehow upset in the restaurant that night. I don't think he'd had a good day on the riverbank and was very forward in telling us that he really did not think much of the English people living and working in his home country. He had a real "they come over here stealing our jobs" chip on his shoulder, particularly with regard to British ex-pat handymen. Averting eyes we made a hasty exit and narrowly avoided a tense diplomatic situation.

The next day, the first proper rain fell, so waterproofs were donned, and the satnav was set for Passio Di Stelvio as the locals call it, but soon to be renamed Steve's Pass by Ian. The TV programme Top Gear introduced me to the Stelvio Pass some years earlier and it has been logged in my memory bank ever since, hoping I would one day get the chance to ride it. Clarkson & Co hadn't mentioned the marvellous Passo Gavia though that we had to ride along first, and which was really enjoyable in itself.

Thankfully, the rain had stopped by the time we reached the start of the pass as it is made up of a tight, steep-sided single-track road which as we ascend, gives glorious views of the valley below and when we reached the top there was still a lot of snow on the ground too. The three of us finally arrive at the summit of the world famous Stelvio Pass and we receive a big cheer from the impressed (or should that be stupefied?) bikers and the two scooter riders already there.

The mountain has two quite different sides. The Stilfs (Stelvio) side is much more open and the pass winds its way down a huge mountain with fantastic scenery and loads of twisty hairpin turns. Looking down on the famous view, I wasn't disappointed by what was still to come. Solid Air's burning clutch would have a much easier time on the way down with the brakes taking over the reins, holding the scooter back when needed as I dashed along the road, down towards the bottom of the pass.

STELVIOPASS
3 Km
BORMIO
dello Stelvio
70
SS38
P.so dello Stelvio
BORMIO

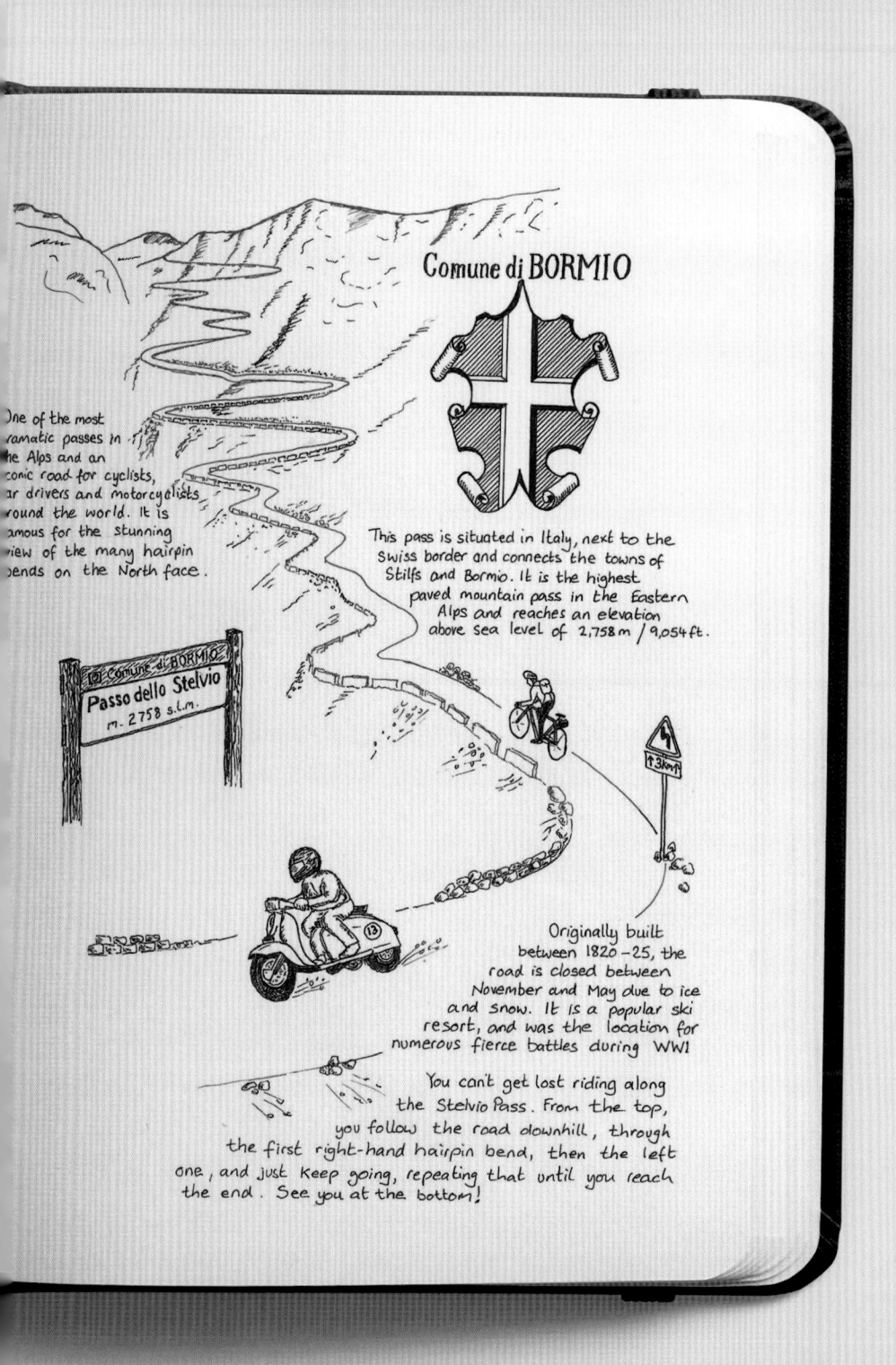

One of the most dramatic passes in the Alps and an iconic road for cyclists, car drivers and motorcyclists around the world. It is famous for the stunning view of the many hairpin bends on the North face.

Comune di BORMIO

This pass is situated in Italy, next to the Swiss border and connects the towns of Stilfs and Bormio. It is the highest paved mountain pass in the Eastern Alps and reaches an elevation above sea level of 2,758m / 9,054ft.

Comune di BORMIO
Passo dello Stelvio
m. 2758 s.l.m.

↑3km

Originally built between 1820-25, the road is closed between November and May due to ice and snow. It is a popular ski resort, and was the location for numerous fierce battles during WWI.

You can't get lost riding along the Stelvio Pass. From the top, you follow the road downhill, through the first right-hand hairpin bend, then the left one, and just keep going, repeating that until you reach the end. See you at the bottom!

Euro Rally scooter legshield banners

152

Nearly at the top, with Andy Neville and Ian Flynn

See you at the bottom!

With a call of "see you at the bottom" to Andy and Ian, I'm off. Twisting the throttle open I rapidly descend the mountain, accelerating towards the bends, approaching wide before braking, tipping the scooter in towards the apex, then sighting the next hairpin and accelerating to do it all over again. The road surface is not in as good a condition as you would think for such a famous road, and potholes, patches of repaired tarmac and loose gravel litter the route. There is also the oncoming traffic and cyclists slavishly pedalling uphill, that must be taken into account. Even though full concentration is needed to connect the multiple hairpins along the route, I snatch quick glances at the famous view as I snake my way down the mountainside, and what a view it is, one that will stay with me for a long time. The downhill ride is far easier and with the help of gravity, far swifter than the uphill slog so the thrill is soon over. My pulse is racing as I pull over when the road levels out and wait for the other two. I park up, remove my gloves and helmet to catch my breath and take in the glorious view until they come back into sight, ambling along at their own sedate and genteel pace but wearing the same ear to ear grin.

At the bottom of the Stelvio Pass, before saying goodbye to Andy and Ian

At the bottom of the pass, I say a fond farewell to my riding companions then head off in one direction as they head home in another. Soon after I had to have a serious talk with myself. I would have thought that after all my years of riding that I would have learnt by now that if it looks like rain, stop and put on some waterproofs. But no, I soldier on through what started off as light and unthreatening occasional rain drops that eventually becomes a full on deluge. My decision of "don't stop, it's clearing up over there" was to be my biggest misjudgement of the trip.

Planning my route at home on my laptop, I had not zoomed in close enough on the map when selecting the waypoints, then I unwittingly transferred the incorrect route onto my satnav. Now, I found myself being misdirected up the side of a mountain that I did not need to go up, and into a torrential thunderstorm. I persevered through rivers of water heading downhill towards me and shear drops of hundreds of feet to the side of me. After quite a distance, and now feeling that something is not right, through my headset I receive the instruction "You have reached your destination, turn around and follow the road ahead." What? It took me a few moments to work out what had happened, but it was now too late. Soaked to the skin from the storm and furious with myself and the satnav, I obediently follow the instructions given and head downhill in the dark and the rain, soaking wet and cursing to myself at full volume inside my crash helmet.

Having wrongly sent myself up a huge mountain in a thunderstorm, with forked lightning and torrential rain all around me, I arrive at the night's stop soaked, hungry and cold and shivering uncontrollably while I try to get the German staff to understand, with my limited knowledge of their language, that I needed somewhere to dry my clothing ready for the next day's ride.

Rain followed, and a lot of it, but I was more prepared for it this time. The next couple of days were a bit of a slog but all part of the journey and the sun thankfully returned in France. Riding through beautiful countryside and towns with names forever associated with World War One, I could not help but wonder at the horrific events of a long time ago. A relaxing lunch and timely progress with an overnight hotel stop before heading home the next day puts me in good spirits. But plans do not always work out as hoped for. I hear some horrible engine noises; the scooter runs but sounds like a bag of nails in a cement mixer then stops. There is nothing for it but to get the tools out, investigate the problem and try to fix it. I strip down the top end of the engine but don't find an obvious problem, so everything is put back together, the scooter starts and seems okay. I reload and set off again. But it's not to be. Remember that potential mechanical heart transplant I mentioned earlier? Well, that became very real. With one more day left of riding through France the heart of the engine, the crank, breaks and throws in the towel. The time has come to test out my breakdown service cover. A night in a different hotel to the one I had planned is followed the next morning by a dash in a French taxi (scary) to pick up a hire car in the morning, but I'm soon homeward bound and arrive only a few hours later than expected. My scooter has been taken away on the recovery vehicle and will arrive home in a few weeks.

On this trip I travelled along some fantastic roads, through six countries, and attempted to speak the language in every one of them. I camped every night but one, saw some beautiful countryside, ate delicious food, met brilliant people, and made new friends. I rode over 2000 miles on a 30+ year old scooter, much to the amusement and admiration of onlookers. Used over 200 litres of fuel and six litres of two-stroke oil, fried a set of clutch plates, wore out a rear tyre, and performed life-saving surgery on an air filter before Solid Air decided to hitch a lift home on a recovery truck (Reims was far enough so it seemed, lazy sod). Despite the breakdown bringing the ride to an early end, I would not have changed a thing.

SPAIN 2018

Abejar in the Soria region of northern Spain was the destination for the 29th Euro Lambretta. From Calais, the round trip totalled around 2,500 miles and I would be travelling solo again but meeting Andy and Ian from Bristol at the rally as well as whoever else turned up along the way.

I left home and the early mist in Cambridge soon gave way to a beautiful blue sky splattered with cotton wool clouds while the Eurotunnel gods were looking down on me and waved me straight onto the train. The French population was enjoying a quiet Sunday, so I was left alone to wander off the beaten track and enjoy some beautiful roads and scenery, ending up at a camp site next to the river Seine.

The next day, some gremlins appeared to keep me on my toes in the form of an uncooperative satnav, a pothole picking a fight with my exhaust and a close shave with a 6ft long flying leylandii branch falling off the back of a lorry, but overall, it was a good day despite these minor inconveniences. The roads were not so much fun to ride though, a lot straighter, but that did help me catch up after being delayed fixing the exhaust. I thought I was doing well travelling across France and into Spain on my scooter, until I got chatting to a fella at that night's campsite who was spending a few months walking from his home in Switzerland to La Rochelle on the west coast of France. That would have given him anywhere between 500 and 700 miles to cover. He was taking it easy and making it up as he went along. I liked the approach he took to his trip, going with the flow and getting a really good look at the country he was travelling across as he went.

Replacing a broken exhaust gasket

Time for tea

Some of the remains at Oradour-sur-Glane

Some years ago in a newspaper magazine, I read an article about a town near Limoges with an incredibly sad and traumatic history. Oradour-sur-Glane is a small town surrounded by rural countryside and enjoyable riding roads that took me past open fields and through forests to reach the town. With its horrific story, wandering the streets and abandoned buildings is a very sobering experience. Men, women, and children were indiscriminately murdered in World War II by the Waffen SS over a weekend when they passed through. Few survived and after the war it was decided that all the buildings should be left as they stood, creating a memorial to the townspeople and the horrors that the soldiers inflicted on them in the name of war. I walked the grounds of this martyred village in an eery hush and at the same time was filled with a sense of shock and awe at the atrocities that people are capable of. Only so much can be conveyed by reading an account of the events that took place there in 1944, words cannot recreate how your senses and emotions will respond to wandering the deserted and time-locked ruins. I return to my scooter and leave, heading for my next overnight stop.

In front of the bullring at Mont de Marsan   Wild horses

I received a warm welcome from the campsite owners and their dogs at La Brugere, close to Bergerac. It felt like I have my own personal campsite with no one else there, so I set up my tent overlooking a sloping grass meadow and peaceful woodland. The only sounds I could hear were birds and insects and I enjoy the peace and solitude while I eat some bread and smelly French cheese. There's thunder in the air and before long the heavens have opened as a storm of orchestral proportions unleashes its fury. I had faith in my tent keeping water out from above but what with the noise of the rain and the risk of flooding I decided to up sticks and move camp to the shower block, bedding down there for the night. In the morning, while sorting out my gear I opened a pannier to notice a few drops of liquid on the waterproof trousers that I had put inside. I was grateful for a narrow escape having left my panniers out in the open, but I had not closed the bag top securely enough. Taking the trousers out, I unfolded them only to see about half a pint of fresh rainwater pour out! Thankfully, there was no water damage to any of the other contents, so after packing everything back up then checking and retightening the exhaust manifold nuts after Monday's pothole incident, I made a leisurely start for my last outward day in France. I enjoyed miles of fast curvy country N-Roads with a few exceptionally long straight up and down stretches, where the French road builders obviously felt it was easier to draw a straight line between A and B, then simply lay down a strip of tarmac regardless of any obstructions.

It's amazing the number of places that I pass through, or ride near that have a famous food or drink connection; Bergerac, Limosin, Burgundy, Armagnac, Roquefort to name a few and it makes me hungry. Spain is getting near; a lot of the road signs are in the Basque language and there is a bullring in Mont de Marsan. Bullfighting is not what I call a fair fight, but it is a very popular and traditional event in the area. Surely the bull should get a couple of swords strapped to its horns to even up the fight though, in the name of fairness?

On the last day before I reach Abejar, I had a frustrating start and wasted an hour going nowhere fast. The satnav kept getting confused and I kept trying to unsuccessfully second guess the route that I should be following. It would have been easier to pull over and sort the problem out properly, but once I stopped wasting time and got back on to the correct route that is soon forgotten. The road I had chosen to take through this part of the Pyrenees was fantastic, hairpin followed hairpin as I climbed up into the mountains with sheer drops of hundreds of feet to the side of me, and wonderful scenery if I dared to steal a glance, but I decided to take the safer option and stopped a couple of times to soak up the views. Creeping up the mountain I'm easily overtaken by a lone BMW motorcycle tourer. I pass a group of horses wandering along the road and verge, large bells hanging round their necks ringing their presence to their owner and hopefully to road users. I stopped to take a few photographs and they looked at me as if to say, "what do you think you are looking at?"

Downhill is easier and the scooter is loving it. I catch up with the BMW and stick with him. He keeps looking in his mirrors worriedly, trying to work out how I caught him up maybe? I must have really spooked him as after a while he pulled over and let me pass. I ride into Pamplona and look for somewhere in the old town to have a coffee when two other Lambrettas pull up. I meet Dave and Mark (Captain Pugwash on the LCGB forum) from Liverpool and spend the next half hour enjoying their company. They come from very close to where my dad was born and Mark reassures me that the memory I have of dolphins swimming in the local public swimming baths, from when I was a kid and visiting grandparents, was not some strange dream but did actually happen. Health and Safety? Pah! Not needed in the 1970s.

We say farewell and I leave the city and straight away find myself riding up more big hills. On one side the landscape is quite flat for some way into the distance but on the other it is a sheer rocky escarpment that runs for miles across the top of this area. I stop and watch in amazement as dozens of huge eagles, or maybe vultures, soar freely in the sky.

I ride onwards through Logroño then onto the last stretch of road that leads to Abejar, and what a road it was. Travelling through a national park for around 50 miles, the road is lined by tall sandstone cliffs, mountains, and gorges. The satnav misbehaves again. I end up riding through Soria then run out of petrol. I top up with the spare fuel I carry and then ride on to the rally campsite, where I pull up and unexpectedly catch sight of Andy Cunningham and Trevor Peat from Cambridge. After a quick chat I am invited to pitch my tent next to theirs.

The gala meal, Gary and Jo Smyth (L) Trevor and Andy (R)

Inside the town walls of Calatanazor

The next day, Friday is a relaxed day; I do a few little jobs on the scooter followed by the usual drinking and dancing in the evening. Saturday involves a wet ride with friends into Soria for some tapas, followed by a

The view approaching the historic town of Calatanazor

drier ride to a tiny, centuries old, fortified city called Calatanazor, Arabic for "Castle of Vultures" apparently. I climbed the old tower where I look down below onto "La Valle de la Sangre" (the Valley of Blood) which was named after an 11th century battle. True to its name, I watched vultures soaring in the skies around the city walls and spot them nesting in nearby cliffs. I ride back to the campsite to get scrubbed up for the gala dinner later that evening and the last night before I head back towards home. That is probably a good thing, three nights of drinking, dancing and late nights is about enough for me.

The first day of the return leg was quite eventful. Loads of great riding on quiet and scenic winding roads. Sadly, the road surface of one long stretch was particularly poor and could only be described as scabby at best. I pass lovely little Spanish villages tucked away in the middle of nowhere, stopping at one for a coffee and was entertained by some local kids playing football in the street. Occasionally they all stop and pick the ball up when a car drives past, just as me and my childhood mates would have done many years before.

Time for coffee *Jumpers for goalposts, or a garage door*

My two-wheeled saviours, José and Beatrice   The Estación Internacional de Canfranc

The scooter appeared to be drinking petrol like it was going out of fashion. I had already run completely dry, filled the tank with the spare 2 litres I carry and then emptied the tank of that too. Looking on the satnav, I saw that the nearest petrol station was about three miles away. If that was not enough the heavens just happened to open at that precise moment, accompanied by thunder and lightning, dropping biblical amounts of water right on top of me. It was my lucky day though. I flagged down two approaching bikes and was rescued by a wonderful gentleman called José, who shot off on his Yamaha Tmax for some petrol, leaving me chatting with his English-speaking daughter Beatrice in the shelter of a farmer's barn. I made two friends out of strangers there and a few days later I was able to repay the favour by helping a young French lad stopped by the side of the road who had also run out of petrol.

Next it was onto visit the abandoned Estación Internacional de Canfranc in the Pyrenees. This railway station was completed in 1928 then closed and abandoned in 1970. It's an amazing sight with its platform measuring 200 metres and is a beautiful building constructed on a mammoth scale. It held a prominent position during both the Spanish Civil War and World War II. Being of strategical importance, it was a major route for transporting materials and smuggling as well as providing a route of escape for Jews and allied soldiers into Spain.

From where I had filled up earlier to my overnight stop it rained, a lot! As the weather forecast predicted the rain to continue through the night, I treated myself to a room in a hostel on the edge of Pyrenees rather than camping. The next day the weather was brighter and clearer, but most importantly dry, and I had a memorable day of riding through the mountains after a spot of maintenance on Solid Air. When I arrived at the hostel the previous night, the engine was running very lumpy at low speeds while the cylinder head temperature also started to creep up, according to the gauge. Before breakfast I whipped off the cylinder head to look at the join with the cylinder barrel. I couldn't see any obvious leaks but then I noticed that one of the barrel studs was a touch loose. With the stud retightened and the engine back together, I set off again with my fingers crossed against any further complications.

Riding into the Pyrenees, I was met with stunning and beautiful scenery. Mile upon mile of amazing roads up to an elevation of nearly 2000m, this change of height does play havoc with the scooter's carb settings though, making riding more difficult, but I soldier on along tiny roads heading further up and into the clouds. Visibility is poor and keeps my speed right down which is just as well because of the sheer drops to the side that come into view as I ride through a gap in the clouds. At one point, the meanest looking cows loom out of the mist and wander along the roads, bells clanging as they saunter in front of me, they do not seem to appreciate my presence and give me looks of sheer scorn as I ride past.

Tea with a view

Not much to see here

Don't look down!

Somewhere in the Spanish Pyrenees

Arriving back in France, I camped on the outskirts of Lourdes and was keen to have a look around. I walked into the town knowing that it is of huge importance to Catholics and a place of pilgrimage for many. Due to a supposed vision of the Virgin Mary over 150 years ago, a huge site has built up attracting many millions of visitors over the years. It was a quiet Monday evening when I arrived, but there were still people paying their respects and walking along to the Grotto where the vision had been seen. The local shops have obviously taken advantage of the situation and there are quite a few places to buy tacky statues of the Virgin Mary along with rosary beads and the like.

The next day was wet again. After leaving Lourdes I rode past what looked like the last resting place for commercial aeroplanes, the aviation version of an elephant's graveyard with lines of immobile planes abandoned in a field. There must be someone in the aviation world who, just like many Lambretta riders, collects broken planes then stores them as they rust away, bastardising them when a difficult to obtain part is needed. A little while later, I had stopped to have some bread and soup for lunch under a sheltered seating area on a terrace next to a river, when one by one the local pétanque crew bowled up, average age about 75, ready to pass a leisurely afternoon with the boys, throwing metal spheres onto the gravel. They were all very perturbed at the rain preventing play but spent their time discussing the merits of my scooter instead, then resorted to playing cards in their club house, before returning home to their wives and domesticity.

In southwest France I stopped off at Angoulême, a small city that hosts an annual classic car race known as the Circuit des Remparts, where drivers speed around the streets of the old town in their historic vehicles, and they don't spare the cars just because they're classics. The old part of the town is on top of a hill with narrow cobbled streets and a road that switches back on itself going down the side of the hill, and I imagine it is a popular place to watch the racing. I would love to come back one day when the races are on. I parked up in one of the small streets there to have my lunch. Despite any Anglo-French hostility there may have been over the years, a few locals wished me "bon appetite" when they see me enjoying my meal, such is their love and enjoyment of food. This sort of moment is something

I relish about travelling on my own or in a small group. A larger group of scooterists will put people off approaching or trying to break into that circle of people for just an instant of human interaction, so moments are missed or possible opportunities of something more are passed by, never to occur.

Back home in England, it is not unusual to get people approaching and reminiscing over their lost youth and experiences on a scooter. It even happened to me in the middle of France on this trip. I sense someone looking at the scooter as I fill up with petrol. "I used to have one of those in the 60s" I hear an expat shout over, "used to go to Brighton and everything!" For a moment it puts a smile on someone's face and reminds them of times long passed.

Continuing my journey, I stay at Saumur for night. I was last there more than 25 years earlier when I toured Normandy and the Loire Valley on my old PX200 with my then wife. Wandering into the town for old times' sake, I find it is still very pleasant, very French (of course) and with a very relaxed atmosphere. The next day I make an early start to squeeze some extra miles in, and ride past the world famous Le Mans race circuit on my way. The first French Grand Prix was held here in 1906 and continues to this day. As in Angoulême, local streets are still closed off so that they can be included as part of the circuit. My timing was poor sadly and I was only able to see preparation for the 24hr race coming up at the weekend, another time maybe?

I was sat enjoying breakfast (porridge with honey and a cup of tea) in the sun on the last day of my trip and was feeling very content. The day shouldn't be a rush and hopefully there will be more pleasing scenery and enjoyable roads to ride. I had booked a later time for the tunnel journey, just in case though. It has been another great journey, everything I had hoped it would be.

About halfway through the ride the front wheel starts weaving and the scooter is handling very strangely. Thinking as I rode along, I couldn't work out why. I had just checked the tyre pressure in Abbeville so they should be ok, the road surface is fine and while it is a bit windy it's not that bad. I pull over to look for the problem. I cannot see anything out of the ordinary with the front wheel, tyre, and forks. All seems okay until I wander round to the back of the scooter. Whilst in my haste to secrete my daily fix of some delicious Kambly Florentin biscuits securely from the prying eyes of HM Customs, well you never know they might be hungry; I had omitted to connect the securing straps properly. I use Rokstraps and highly recommend them, but on this occasion the failure was due entirely to operator error, so their reputation is safe. My waterproof Kappa bag, also recommended, had worked loose of the straps, and was now hanging down behind the scooter's number plate just inches above the road surface, thankfully not touching it though. It was held up by just two clips caught in the plastic eyelets of the bag. I have a chuckle to myself and thanked my lucky stars. Shortly after, I stop for my last roadside cuppa in a lovely village before riding the last 20 miles or so to the tunnel. There was a backlog at customs, but I trundle to near the front of the queue, have a quick chat with the French customs officer about the trip and then head straight for an earlier crossing, happy days, but bloody hell, I am back in England for just two minutes before I have to take evasive action when a couple of cars both decide to go for the same patch of road, smack bang in front of me. It's good to be back, I think? Home and happy, Solid Air is parked up in the comfort of the garage with the weekend off for good behaviour, until Monday comes round, and work beckons again.

POLAND 2019

In true scooter rally style and after much faffing around, I am still busy preparing into the early hours of Saturday morning before battling the wind and rain down to Folkestone to then head towards Zakopane. Bumping into Warren Smith from Guildford and Alan Baker, Kev and Ronnie from London made the delay at Folkestone for the Eurotunnel much more pleasant, before we split up to follow our own planned routes and to do battle with the howling wind. Saturday finished at a lovely, secluded campsite in Belgium where I was invited to join the locals in their delicious BBQ meal along with a few glasses of Leffe, spot on! The barman looked after me, sending me up for seconds and topping up a glass with red wine for me while the lovely lady that booked me onto the site called for me especially when pudding was served. I'm in heaven. A real mixture of roads followed on Sunday, with some good old Belgian roads, dead straight for miles and miles up hill and down dale, then through a national park in Luxembourg where bend followed bend through thickly wooded forest. I rode into Germany in the afternoon where the bikers were out in force but sadly most BMW and Goldwing riders still do not know how to return a wave, that doesn't stop me though.

Stopping overnight at a friendly little campsite smack in the middle of the Moselle wine region at the right time in the year meant I could sample the local tipple on Sunday night, before heading deeper into Germany and then on towards the Czech Republic. A German gentleman, of at least 80 years old, came over to my tent for a chat and reminisced about the scooters he had owned when he was younger, then the following morning he came dashing over to tell me he had been dreaming about the scooters and his youth because of our chat! He had ridden down to Sardinia on his Heinkel Tourist in the 1950s or 60s and the revived memories put a huge smile on his face. He wished me a safe and enjoyable trip before I set off the short distance to the Backerei (bakery) Fleury in Braunberg. The bakery was featured in a Hairy Bikers TV programme and as I make bread; I thought I would pay a quick visit to sample their wares. Sadly, the Master Baker was not there but I left with a delicious loaf of Wrot Brot which, being fermented for 48 hours, makes it very tasty and kept me going all day.

Stocking up at the Bakery

With Bernard from Rudesheim

A good start saw me riding alongside the Moselle River looking for the road I needed to take, only to find it was closed for repairs. After quite a detour I get back on track and find myself riding 60 miles of slow, tedious roads heavy with traffic, a right old schlep. At the end of the boring part, I was sat by the roadside enjoying a coffee when a passing Harley Davidson rider noticed me, slammed on his brakes, and whipping his bike around mounted the pavement to park up and say hello. I spent the next ten minutes talking about bikes, our trips, and the rally with Bernhard from Rudesheim. He was gobsmacked that I had ridden all the way from England and when I told him that I was riding to Zakopane he nearly fell over. He, like the older German gentleman, had also ridden to Sardinia with friends, which makes me think that it must be worth a visit one day.

Later, Solid Air's Quattrini engine was on song when I rode a particularly enjoyable series of bends, connecting them all up beautifully. Then the rain started and continued until I arrived two hours later at the campsite, where I set up my tent and then enjoyed some local beers and a bowl of goulash while waiting for the rain to stop. Tuesday was a cracking day's ride into the Czech Republic. Everything was a little bit more "rustic" there. Plaster fallen from buildings is not always replaced and there are a lot more older buildings. The countryside is beautiful, starting off with packed woodland followed by large open plains, like a smaller version of the American prairies, not that I have ever been there, but you'll know what I mean. Towards Prague the roads are lumpy, and the scooter's exhaust scrapes the tarmac a few times on the bumps. Traffic builds up to normal levels for a large city and after missing the necessary turn a couple of times I eventually find the campsite where I had arranged to meet Andy Neville. Unfortunately, and despite Andy's reassurances of "how many campsites can there be on this little island in the middle of the river in Prague?" it soon becomes clear that there are two, one where I was booked in and another where Andy was booked in. We soon meet up though and caught a ferry over to explore the old city a bit before finding a bar to settle in and enjoying some delicious local beers and tasty pretzels that were hanging from racks on the table, before realising that the snacks were not complimentary as we both thought, bugger.

Andy Neville surrounded by rusting cars

(Left) Andy Neville, Claire and Martin Kightly, (Right) Jo and Gary Smyth

A dull start to the ride took us through the outskirts of Prague the next morning, but this was soon followed by some deliciously smooth tarmac, sweeping bends and hairpins that had Andy beaming from ear to ear inside his crash helmet. Luckily, despite a festival they had planned for the weekend, our next campsite found us some space to pitch our tents. Only we didn't. The evening was beautifully warm and so after a few glasses of beer, a bite to eat and a drop of the local slivovica, we decided against the luxury of canvas and just unpacked the sleeping mats and bags to spend a night under the stars, but not before an impromptu game of "name that tune" using my trusty iPod, with artists ranging from Johnny Cash to We've Got a Fuzzbox and We're Gonna Use It via Freddie Chavez and Bauhaus. An unnaturally early start saw us being woken by sunshine and birdsong before hitting the road at the unheard of time of 8am. We passed a roadside field that had been turned into a graveyard for unwanted cars, where parked up and rusting Skoda's were gradually being hidden from view by the grass and weeds and we saw telegraph poles with stork nests perched on top that really should have had planning permission going by the size of them.

Despite getting hotter and some appalling roads the ride was great. One particular downhill hairpin will remain in the memory for some time though, changing mid bend from silky smooth tarmac to cobbles that must have been through an earthquake, they were that rough and shaken up. Slightly later, my life flashed before me when a carefree tractor driver shot across the road at full speed just yards in front of us, without even a glance in our direction.

We reached Zakopane on Thursday afternoon and settled into our accommodation before heading out to enjoy a few beers on the campsite. There didn't seem to be the usual amount of people present to provide the normal first night buzz. We did however bump into friends from the previous Euro rally in Spain, Gary and Jo Smyth and Martin and Claire Kightly, and had a raucous evening with them before stumbling back to the apartment and a well-earned sleep. Friday was hot and the night was a much livelier occasion with more riders arriving. Saturday was even hotter, but a drop of rain cooled things down just a tiny bit.

Over the weekend, I came to realise a couple of important points that may be of use to others in the future, 1: Polish Road surfaces can be crap (lovely people though) and 2: Andy talks to everyone, and I mean EVERYONE, not good if you are in a hurry. The LCGB repair tent, manned by Andy Vass and Nick Prince, carried out a sterling job all weekend helping riders with their mechanical problems and repairs that needed fixing, hopefully helping them to complete the return journey rather than needing to call breakdown recovery for a lift back to the UK. An evening of drinking, talking, and dancing followed and was enjoyed by all, including a young lad by the name of Dan Reynolds, son of Keith. At only 22 years old he was on his first European trip on a Lambretta, what a way to start his European scooter exploits.

Sunday sees us homeward bound and, after a few tip offs about roadworks, we followed the scenic route to Kraków, which turned out to be an excellent choice. The weather held out for us and there were some wonderful hairpins to negotiate which again Andy loved. We nearly got caught out at one point when taking a left turn, we suddenly saw what looked like a whole village that had turned out in their Sunday best for a street market that took up the whole road, with stalls full of tat for the kids to spend their pocket money on. We slowly weaved our two-stroke way through the bemused crowd and carried on towards the Goodbye Lenin Hostel in Kraków, with its distinctly ironic communist feel. That evening

Three pics from Kraków...

...The House of Beer

...Communist kitsch

...A motley crew

we wandered around the historic parts of the city, through the Jewish Quarter, onto a medieval fair, around the castle and then into the old town. We joined up with some fellow LCGB members for a few drinks, lots of jokes and storytelling that was finished with the traditional post-pub kebab (for me anyway, not so for vegetarian Andy).

We were both interested in visiting the infamous World War II concentration camp at Auschwitz, so took a slight detour along the way. The plan was to park up and have a wander around the site but upon arrival, there was a huge throng of tourists and the coaches that they had disembarked from. I stayed sat on my scooter, crash helmet on, near the end of the infamous train track, looking towards the entrance to the camp. I watched as people took photographs and selfies, and asked myself, because of the way that some of them were behaving, if they fully appreciated the history of the site and whether due dignity was being given. Probably not by some I have to say sadly. After a time, we restarted the scooters turned them around and rode away.

We were riding along what must have been the smoothest tarmacked road in Poland, particularly compared to some of the others where it felt like you were riding a pogo stick, when we noticed a motorcyclist stopped by the kerb. We slowed down and gave the questioning thumbs-up for "Are you okay?" and received the "Yes all's well" wave on but decided to pull over just past him anyway and have a break and a cuppa. While waiting for the kettle to boil we watched the biker on the phone to the recovery company, or so we thought. Then we watched as shortly after a lorry pulls up behind his bike. The biker jumps up into the cab, both driver and biker move into the back of the cab and moments later the biker exits the cab, with a small bag "possibly" containing a white powdery substance. The motorbike accelerates harshly away immediately afterwards, all very interesting. We continued onwards to ride along some of the normal Polish roads (i.e. crap) which brought on Andy's white knuckle and then we diced with a fair number of Polish drivers who thought it was okay to overtake a line of vehicles in a no overtaking zone while approaching blind bends at full pelt, mad!

Somewhere in the planning for this rally, I realised that it would be possible to spend a night in a town called Colditz, home to Colditz Castle where a 1970s television drama was set and was based on the true stories of servicemen trying to escape from a prisoner of war camp for officers in World War II. The castle now finds itself repurposed and welcomes people to stay overnight within its walls but allowing them to leave as and when they wish, quite different to how it must have been as a prison. It has had a smart coat of white paint, been converted into a youth hostel, and looks atmospherically quite different to the black and white war films that I watched as a kid and where it would have provided an ominous and oppressive backdrop. The next day Andy headed off by himself following his route home, and I covered around 250 miles to reach my next stop. Luckily, I managed to skirt around a massive storm and so the waterproofs stayed packed away. I might have dodged that storm but not the one later in the day. Everything was calm on the campsite, but then the apocalypse happened. There was a massive electrical storm right over head with rain and wind to match. I got into my tent, battened down the hatches and waited for it to stop only for the youngsters gathering around a lake next to the campsite, to take their turn to kick up a racket well into the early hours once the storm had cleared.

I planned a visit to Utrecht in the Netherlands to pay a surprise visit on my son Arthur. He had been spending some of his university time there since February, and having not been able to visit before then, I was really looking forward to seeing him, catching up and tasting a few of the local beers with him. On the way, near Arnhem, I passed what looked like a classic car museum only to find that it was actually a showroom of luxury cars for sale. When I say showroom, what I really mean is, four massive floors of the crème de la crème of the classic car world; Lamborghini, Bugatti, Ferrari, Jaguar, MG, Alfa Romeo, Morgan the list just goes on and also included a Lambretta, a Vespa, an NSU and some wonderful motorcycles, my favourite being a beautiful example of a Benelli in-line six-cylinder.

Coming from Cambridge where push bikes are plentiful and famous for it, I am used to seeing a lot of bicycles shooting around a busy city, but not on the level I saw in Utrecht, they are everywhere, never-ending and then you've got all the little mopeds buzzing along the pavements, with no crash helmets on, oh and a sweet smelling herbal aroma coming from the "coffee" shops wafts around the streets.

The beautiful six-cylinder Benelli

For my last overnight stop, what more fitting, than a place in Ghent to prepare for the Belgian Euro rally in 2020? To get there I decided that the motorway would be the best bet, fast and direct. I wanted to have a look around the town and sample the delights of the many Belgian beers on offer there. I took advantage of riding a scooter and filtered through a couple of big traffic jams, one caused by an overturned car, thankfully everyone seemed to be ok. I found my accommodation easily enough, a former monastery and had a quick freshen up before heading into town, where I found crowds of people lounging around the canal side areas, with pavement cafés, a proper old castle right in the middle of the city and even more pushbikes. During a bit of a mosey around I stumbled across some local street art tucked away in a very brightly decorated alley and stopped for a bite to eat at Frites Atelier (a Belgian chip shop) which really hit the spot before heading onto a little pub called the Dulle Griet for some delicious Belgian beers. I was about to wander off back to the hotel when I got chatting to a group of German fellas who had just arrived and sat on the table next to me. This turned out to be both good and bad. Good because they were a friendly bunch, all remarkably interesting in their own way, one a fan of English poetry and another with a similar taste in music to me, that he discovered by listening to the John Peel show on Radio 1, but bad because it involved more beer.

Nearing Utrecht

Two of my new German friends in Ghent

Despite this, I was up and out nice and early, even if with a bit of a thick head. The weather was good but some of the Belgian roads needed a bit of care riding over due to their rough surfaces, but not to the degree of those in Poland thankfully. I kept off the motorway today to enjoy the last stretch of the ride and took a break sat in the sun outside the charming little Café de la Douane, on the French/Belgian border before reaching the Eurotunnel terminal. There was quite a lot of bikes there returning from their trips, and I must admit to always feeling slightly chuffed when bikers find out what we put our poor little machines through in the name of scootering, and their astonishment at what can be achieved with the will. A few hours later I had landed back at home with a warm welcome from both the dog and my wife (in that order) to bring another great trip to an end.

BELGIUM ~~2020, 2021,~~ 2022

Well, 2020 what a year that was. I cannot think of anybody that was expecting it to go quite as it did, no thanks to a world pandemic. Scooter events, along with pretty much everything else, were either massively depleted or non-existent. The annual European road trip was cancelled, and the Belgian organisers were massively disappointed at not being able to welcome everyone to their Lambretta Jamboree.

And 2021 was pretty much the same, but then in 2022…

Talk about cutting it fine. No European Lambretta rallies for the past two years because of COVID-19 and for one reason or another, I had not applied for a new passport until extremely late in the day. Due to the Passport Office being overwhelmed with the post-COVID-19 demand I just couldn't get an appointment for a quick passport for love nor money, so going to the Post Office for a digital application was my final clutching at straws plan. Now I just had to wait with my fingers crossed. The weekend before my hopeful departure, the mischievous scooter gremlins were busy at work while I was prepping my scooter in the hope that my new passport would arrive in time. I would complete one job only to find another, what with a cracked exhaust support bracket and an air leak that needed sealing off, so on and so on. The preceding days to departure were tense and frustrating but where there is the will there is a rally to attend, and with the help of a friendly biker workshop with welding equipment and my persistent approach to get Solid Air ready, I was eventually all set for departure. But still no passport, will I be going? Who knows? I had already had to disappointingly shorten the trip for other reasons. But then at 8am on Monday morning I receive a delivery notification followed at 8:15 by an unable to deliver notification. Is this trip meant to be? I have wondered many times if fate is taking a hand in my scooter journey. But it does look like fate might actually be in my favour. One brand new passport is delivered and received the next day, one day before I am due to leave, what a relief! Now, with all systems go, the plan is to meet Andy, posh scooterboy Ian and Martin Lovell from Bristol, in France for an overnight stop before riding into Belgium to meet up with all those crazy scooter folk that have not been able to venture into Europe for three years, until now… hurrah!

An uneventful ride down to Folkestone and the Eurotunnel was followed by some wonderfully smooth, twisty, and quiet French roads. The weather looked good for the trip, dry and warm, and would stay that way until it was time to turn for home on Sunday morning. The overnight stop was a small campsite near Saint Quentin where I was due to meet the Bristol Lambretta Club folk. Arriving in the early evening I was able to visit the local Intermarche supermarket for some beers as well as bread, ham and cheese for my evening meal and which became the theme for the trip as we built our diet around the staples of booze, cheese, ham, and bread. The BLC Road Crew finally arrived later in the evening with Andy's Li, Doris, doing an admirable impression of a bomber plane with an exhaust that was well past its best. Their late arrival sadly deprived them of the necessary intake of alcohol, so a sensible evening saw our small group all fresh and raring to go in the morning. The obligatory stop at a French marketplace cafe for drinks and nibbles was taken, and whilst there a French version of the Chuckle Brothers rolled up on their little mopeds. The first had a hilariously high-pitched voice and complete lack of awareness that we didn't have a clue what he was saying to us, and when his mate, or maybe his brother, tried to drag him away, he had a matching squeak of a voice too. We were all goggle eyed and trying not to laugh too excessively at the moment, a perfect little vignette of the type of experiences and people that can make these European trips so memorable. Shortly after this we bumped into some riders from Devizes Sweet Sensation SC and the two groups would leapfrog each other along the route, stopping for pics at the French/Belgian border together, enjoying the wonderfully curvy and hilly roads of the Ardennes region and then all arriving in Libramont ready to make camp and stock up with supplies of beer, ham, bread and cheese.

Border crossing, with Bristol Lambretta Club and Devizes Sweet Sensation SC

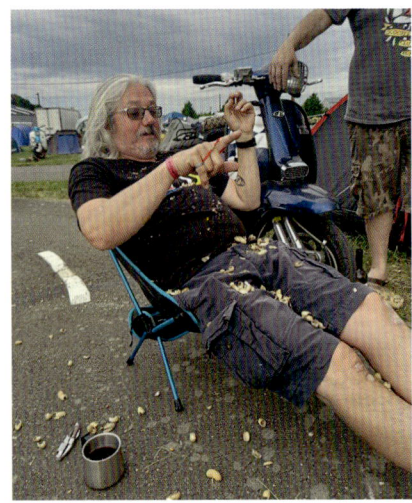

Ian and his exploding nuts

The Belgium Lambretta Club have experienced their fair share of frustrations trying to organise this rally, but Erwin Tumkiewicz and his crew were all hard at work over the weekend either on the gate, dishing out goody bags or feeding the massed ranks of hungry scooter riders (along with some LCGB volunteers). Well done to all! Friday lunch time found us all a bit peckish, so we wandered into the local town for lunch. Pizza was mentioned but then someone clever indicated that would just be another combination of cheese, bread, and ham and maybe something different would be fun? So, we ventured on and thankfully stumbled on a delightful little Greek restaurant called La Creta. The staff were welcoming, the food delicious and the wine was flowing. There was also a large bowl of complimentary Haribo MAOM sweets, which were rapidly depleted once discovered, and these were soon followed by liberal doses of Cognac and Poire Alsace. We were well on the way at this point but where to we did not quite know. Post lunch merriment continued at the nearby Diamond's bar with a few glasses of delicious Leffe beer (oh dear) and on the way back to camp, Ian had a traumatic experience with a bag of exploding monkey nuts, which I am sure the Devizes mob had booby trapped to discharge its contents over him as he innocently opened them.

The evening and following day continued in much the same way, consuming the staples of bread, ham, and cheese along with copious amounts of alcohol, which had a hilarious effect on late night discussions around our tents, where people owning varying accents from around the UK and European mainland stopped by to join in the conversation. Friday lunchtime was so good that we felt compelled to make a second visit to La Creta, which was just as enjoyable as the day before, if a bit more sedate. Perhaps not back in Diamond's bar though? Reports of rally goers drinking the bar dry saw us, and others, head to the Lion Rouge bar for our pre-gala meal drinks.

As the weather people predicted, Sunday was wet, and the amount of rain that afternoon approached biblical standards. But with overnight stops, cross Channel ferries booked, or continuing trips arranged, everyone was decamping and heading off regardless. I ended up riding on the tail of the Manchester Lyons SC for the start of the return journey before finding myself on my own again. Tim Partridge, also a Lyon but riding solo, was following the same route and we both ended up sheltering from the rain at the same petrol stations before finding ourselves camped at the same site in Ypres. We joined forces for a wander around the town taking in a very tasty burger and chips as well as a few more beers, before visiting the Menin Gate for the last post. Monday saw a repeat of the first day's ride to the Eurotunnel, very pleasant, dry and trouble free. Arriving home midafternoon having thoroughly enjoyed myself on this long overdue European trip, I parked Solid Air and crashed out on the sofa, thankful for yet more great scooter experiences to add to the memory bank.

PART 4

WACKY RACES

BRITISH SCOOTER
ENDURANCE CLUB
238

ENDURANCE RACING

When I worked as a motorcycle instructor, training learner riders to pass the two-part motorcycle test and then the Compulsory Basic Training (CBT), I had many opportunities to ride different motorcycles and was lucky enough to spend a day thrashing a Suzuki GS500E around the Brands Hatch race circuit. Being younger, riding quickly was a big draw and speeding around local country roads on my RGV250 or on the way to World Superbike race or motorcycle grand prix, always bought the boy racer out in me and my instructor work mates. But going racing as a competitor never really entered my mind for more than a fleeting moment. Having a young family, it was never going to be possible to take part in a race series over several months in the summer with the massive time and financial commitment that it would demand.

Nearly thirty years later…

Having taken part in scooter endurance racing on the European mainland, Keith Terry (former co-owner of the well-known scooter shop Kegra Racing, engine tuner, scooter racer and World Record Holder) wondered why this form of racing did not take place back home in the UK. Rather than leave it at that, he decided to set up the British Scooter Endurance Club (BSEC) and organise races using small go-kart and pit bike type circuits. Keith really wanted to give the opportunity to normal road going riders, who could not commit the time and money that a season of racing requires, to thrash a classic scooter around a track. A full licence holding road going scooterist could use their normal scooter if it met certain basic requirements, and with a few other like-minded friends, they could form a team if they could buy and then fit into a set of motorcycle leathers, which is not always as easy as it sounds for a middle-aged scooterboy.

The circuits that have been used so far are a lot smaller than somewhere like the well-known and popular Cadwell Park or Mallory. They have a high number of turns in a lap to make the racing lively and also allow an incredibly unobstructed view of the circuit, which combined with a vast array of riders out on the track at the same time, makes for a great spectator experience too. The teams have a choice of four categories to choose from, allowing them to enter anything from a completely road legal scooter piloted by riders with no track experience all the way up to a full on, full-bodied, race prepared machine ridden by people holding current race licences and with many years race experience. The format is simple and effective but provides lots of scope for team tactics as well as things to unexpectedly change. In an eight-lap sprint race for instance, a crash or a breakdown could mean the end of your race, in an endurance race there is the opportunity for the rider to make their way to the pits and repair bent bodywork, change riders, fix mechanical problems, even to change an engine or the whole scooter if necessary. These occasions would cause time delays or lap penalties, in the case of an engine or scooter swap, but potentially the team could keep the scooter out on the track enjoying the experience and getting excellent value for their money, even if it puts them out of the running for a trophy.

The race meeting starts on the Friday with a practice session where cobwebs can be blown away and any scooter niggles sorted out. Saturday morning will bring an early rise, with bacon butties for breakfast if you're lucky (and not vegetarian) followed by another practice session where the lap times will decide where a team lines up on the start grid. To get the race underway, all scooters are lined up with engines running and throttles being blipped by a team member, decimating the ozone layer directly above the circuit with two-stroke fumes. All the team's first riders will be poised on the opposite side of the track waiting for Keith to drop the start flag. When he does, they dash across the track just like the racers at Le Mans, and jump onto their machine to hopefully get their race underway without colliding with another scooter.

So far, the races have been either of six or eight hours duration and the aim is for each team to complete as many laps as possible in that time, hopefully avoiding breakdowns, accidents, and cockups. It is not necessary to have the fastest or the best looking machine on the track, what is important is to keep the machine "shiny side up" while the riders take turns to clock up as many laps as they can in the time available. It sounds easy but it's not, however much preparation or training is done, nobody knows what will happen on the day and that is one of the things that makes this type of racing so much fun!

TEESSIDE 2020

One night in September 2019, my phone pings. A message comes through from Nigel and Paul, two fellas I've shared a few drinks and laughs with on some LCGB Events. They had spectated at the first BSEC endurance race the previous year and wanted to have a go themselves. Following a discussion in their local pub, The Crossing, they decided to contact me with the message "Wanna make a team to do some endurance racing next year?" and before my brain had really thought about it in an adult, informed and reasoned way, I had replied "YEAH! Too Right I do! When?" And so, Privateer Racing was formed, and race preparations began. Our poor phones were sent into overdrive as our heads ran away with us and plans were made. A scooter was sourced, purchased and came to be known as Billy. The team was expanded with David Clark joining as the non-riding responsible adult and Viv McCann as our friendly spanner wielding Viking. Leathers were bought and then rebought when they didn't fit, by more than one member of the team. Our places on the grid at Whilton Mill and Teesside were booked.

Anticipation was building amongst everyone in the BSEC Facebook group. Then along came COVID-19. That was not part of the plan. Keith Terry, his team and the racers were all left frustrated with this new world, but no one had any choice in the matter and so race one at Whilton Mill was cancelled. Keith had the great idea of holding the first event slightly differently (with no actual racing taking place) and prizes were presented in a virtual custom show style where Billy received his first trophy for Best Lockdown Scooter of 2020. Nationally, fingers were being crossed for Teesside to go ahead and across the country and in true scooter rally style teams prepared their machines right up to the last minute. Spectators were allowed, then they weren't, but thankfully, despite the dastardly virus's best efforts and a local spike Teesside was on, and Privateer Racing were about to lose their racing cherry. Reality was hitting home, and the nerves were building. We arrived at the track, set up camp and prepared to race. Friday night's practice was a little bit shaky to start with but on our second outings we all started to settle down. Race day came. Pre-race qualifying showed up an uncooperative brake pedal retaining clip that needed a quick fix and then we found ourselves in position 13 on the starting grid. We were as ready as we were going to be.

Privateer Racing –
L to R Nigel Sleightholm, Dave Clark, Paul Thomson and me

An unscheduled stop during a red flag at Teesside

The Le Mans Start came. Paul, with his worn out knees, hobbled across the track towards Nigel and Billy the race bike, then in a cloud of two-stroke they were gone. We were racing and 2020 was not a complete failure after all. This racing lark is great, but it is not without its risk. The race soon had a short red flag stop for an injured rider who had unintentionally pressed the eject button, then another team crashed and suffered a broken set of handlebars but admirably replaced them and got back out on the track to continue. The second red flag later in the race was more serious though. The rider, Dave Taylor of Team Challenger Equipe, suffered some very serious injuries and all the riders had a long stop out on the track while he was attended to.

The further into the race we got, the more we settled down. With us all finding our lines and braking points easier, lap times were improving, and The Privateers found themselves with the lead and a four lap advantage in the Club Class right up until 10 minutes from the end. Then I bin it! Going for an overtake that maybe I shouldn't have, and rather than collide with the other rider, I head for the kerb and grass but there's a pothole on my line that I had not expected. I hit the hole and lose control of Billy, hitting the tarmac hard. I'm cursing myself, all I had needed to do was bring it home, but I got over ambitious in the excitement of racing. Wandering over to the fallen bike I can't see much damage and before I know it

Keith Terry has stood Billy up and is shouting at me "You've got about 10 minutes left, get back to the pits!" Billy will not start so back I go, pushing the scooter the short distance along the side of the track to the pits. The team do an admirable job of straightening and restarting the scooter then I am off out again with some ground to make up. The next thing I know is the chequered flag is being waved and we are on the slow down lap back to the pits. The smiles, fist pumps and hugs tell me that Privateer Racing held on to take first place in Club Class in their first race, unbelievable!

WHILTON MILL 6HR 2022

For two seasons I rode with Privateer Racing and in 2021 we raced at both Whilton Mill and Teesside. Together we found a way through the period of COVID-19 lockdown and uncertainty with humour and the anticipation of racing. Just before a world pandemic threw everybody's life into chaos and turmoil, we had started a Thursday night virtual pub night because of the distance that separated us, which proved to be perfect timing for what was pending. I can safely say that being a part of Privateer Racing, the laughs and the moral support provided by these friends and the excitement of the race, was one of the things that got me through the hardest two years of my life following the breakup of my marriage, and I will always be grateful for that.

Sadly, as with many things in life though, good things come to an end and in 2022 I decided to put Team Solid Air together with myself, best mate Viv McCann, and Shane Hunsdale riding with Andrea McCann and Andrew Scott helping with pit lane re-fuelling, tea making duties and moral support. We completed our first race at Whilton Mill, using my road scooter Solid Air, but were dogged by a few small problems that prevented us from being competitive on the day. Despite the race gremlins, spirits were up and kept up with a few beers in the bar that night, before heading home the next day to restart race preparations. Not long after, fellow Euro Lambretta rally goer Gary Smyth was recruited and joined us to race at the next Teesside meeting.

TEESSIDE 8HR 2022

As always, and despite all good intentions, we were preparing for this race right up to the drop of the flag. Shane's newly built engine had put up major resistance against being used for eight hours straight and despite some heroic efforts by him the engine finally won that particular race. Solid Air was drafted back into race use but there was a problem. The engine needed a new piston and that only arrived on the Wednesday and needed fitting on Thursday so that Shane could collect the complete scooter to then drive up to Teesside on Friday. No pressure there then.

To make things just a tad more complicated, Viv had a wedding in Glasgow on the Friday so could not attend that night's practice and I was attending my son's graduation ceremony in Norwich, nothing like an easy ride is there? Viv would join in as soon as he arrived on Saturday, and I would leave home near Cambridge just after 3am to arrive in time for race day practice. Shane is held up on Friday by traffic delays and sadly neither he nor Gary get any time out on track because of that and electrical issues with Solid Air. At one point on Friday night Shane experiences a drastic loss of blood sugar so goes majorly wobbly due to his hectic run up to the race, but thanks to Gary and another racer, Colin Stringer of Rushden Lambretta Club, he is looked after and returned to normal after getting some food inside him.

I arrive at 7am on race day and we set about fitting a replacement stator plate before breakfast and hallelujah, Solid Air finally starts. In the meantime, Gary and his wife Jo are the hosts with the most and supply pre-race sustenance in the form of sausage and bacon baps and tea which is gratefully received. Finally, three quarters of the team get to ride round the track for pre-race practice. There is some final fettling needed with the clutch cable and we end up last out onto the grid to take our place for the start. Because the kickstart is removed for the race we need to bump start the engine into life. Heading to take our place on the starting grid, one of us is running along pushing the scooter while the other sits on the scooter at the controls for the bump start. This proves troublesome and challenging work, and we cannot get the engine to fire up, not what is needed to start a race, until I realise that the engine kill switch is not fully disengaged. With relief the problem is fixed quickly, the engine sparks into life and I position the scooter on the side of the track. Keith Terry waves his flag with a flourish, Shane ambles across the track towards me in the Le Mans start (frankly he is knackered from pushing the scooter) and the race is finally on.

Shane has a good steady start in his first session and comes back into the pits to hand over to Gary, who soon settles down and finds his racing feet again, consistently dropping his lap times. Towards the end of his session, he takes a tumble but is thankfully uninjured, the scooter just needs a new clutch lever. While he is in the pits, we decide to replace the slipping clutch plates as they are hampering speed along the straight and may not last the whole race. Due to the clutch, we are out of the running but there is plenty more fun to be had and we are still racing, it will take a lot more than that to stop us.

I get out on track and about 45 minutes in, when accelerating out of a corner, the rider in front of me appears to give a quick dab on his brakes. I touch my front brake once but realise that's not enough to avoid running into the back of his scooter when he brakes a second time, so I brake again but harder. My front wheel locks, I slam into the tarmac and find myself trying to work out which way is up before floundering over to the tyre wall to gather my thoughts. I must say thanks here to Brook Northey of #55 Team Numpties who looked after me for a few moments and settled me down after my tumble. Back in the paddock, Solid Air is straightened and put straight back out on track.

Viv and Andrea had finally arrived from Glasgow, and following my crash Viv gets straight out onto the track with, admirably, no time at all for any practice. He also leaves the track briefly at one point but keeps upright with the aid of his ankle in between the scooter and the gravel. After his stint, he ends up hobbling around for a bit seeking the attention of the female support team, but unsurprisingly finds none. Everyone gets out for another go in the severe heat we are experiencing, and the second half carries on with far less mishaps. All four riders settle into completing lap after lap, enjoying the whole experience and after eight hours the race finishes and we are elated to reach that point despite all the obstacles put in our way. Beers are opened, hugs are shared, and photographs taken before the traditional end of race presentations by Keith and his team.

I must point out here how amazing my Team Solid Air mates are. They are out to race purely for the hell of it and happy to go along with my race plan, which is to do as best as we can but to have a bloody good laugh along the way, regardless of what happens or where we finish. Shane had a hectic race build up with little sleep, and with only 20 minutes practice he was first out on track and straight on it. Gary had not ridden the scooter before, had not ridden at Teesside since the first BSEC race three years earlier and straight away was reducing his times lap by lap. Viv travelled down from Glasgow that same morning, had no practice time at all and went straight out on track to get on with the job in hand. What more can I ask and what better way for a group of old fellas to spend their time than tear arsing a poor little scooter around a track in searing heat along with a grid full of likeminded people!

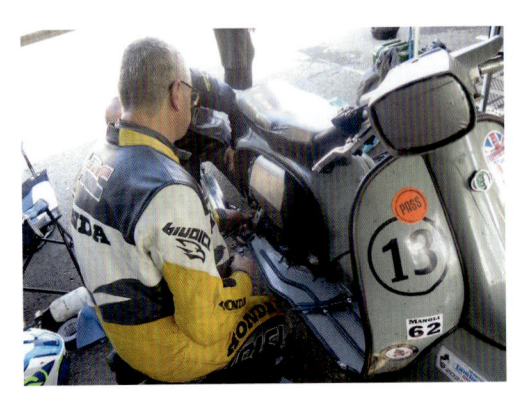

Solid Air needing adjustments at Teesside

A new crash helmet was needed!

TEESSIDE 6HR 2022

Over just three seasons I have learnt that however much planning and preparation is put in before a race, there is always something overlooked or some pesky gremlin lurking deep in the bowels of a scooter engine. For the third BSEC endurance event of 2022, we were back at Teesside Autodrome for a six hour race. The plan was to ride up to Viv's workshop on the Thursday to do some small jobs on the scooter, to have a catch-up with him and Andrea in the evening and then give the scooter a final check over on Friday morning in preparation for the race, before heading over to the track, which is only a 30 minute ride away and should leave plenty of time to spare. As easy as that, or so we thought.

The ride across the Fen roads between home and Peterborough and then the slog all the way up the A1 at a steady 60 to 65mph towards Darlington was uneventful. The closer I was getting, the more I was willing Solid Air to complete that first leg without any problems and barring a pothole jolting the spark plug cap off, I arrived at the workshop midafternoon. Once we'd had a chat and a cuppa we set to work on the scooter. There were a few straight forward jobs that needed doing to get race ready;

swap the normal road tyres for a pair of grippy Mitas MC35s, remove the spare wheel and sprint rack, change the gearbox oil, investigate the noisy exhaust and remove the emergency two litre bottle of petrol under the side panel, leaving just the kickstart and centre stand to be taken off at the race track. No major problem there, so we set to work, chatting away discussing whether the rain will hold off for the race, team tactics and so on.

Everything was ticking along nicely. I decided to check the rear brakes shoes out while we were at it. I found that they needed replacing and while a new pair were being fitted Viv became concerned about some play in the layshaft. The rear hub and wheel attach to the splined layshaft which, inside the engine casing, forms part of the gear box. There should only be a minimal amount of movement between the various components otherwise any excessive play will put unwanted strain on the other engine parts. We both pondered the situation for a few moments, and considering the abuse it will receive on the track, Viv made the decision. "No, we need to have a look inside at the gearbox and see what's going on. Better now than tomorrow in the paddock" and what wise words they were. The clutch side casing was removed and upon inspection we found that the end plate needle bearing had failed and would have very soon caused major problems if left unchecked. Remember what I said about pesky gremlins earlier? Well, here they were. With the problem found, we decided to call it a day and return the next morning with fresh heads and clean hands.

"Fuck! Stair rods, bloomin' stair rods! That's what they call rain like this up here in Darlo, I haven't seen rain like this for ages" was Viv's sentiment on opening the curtains the following morning, and stair rods it certainly was. How long was it going to last? How would it affect the race? Questions we couldn't answer. The weather forecast on Andrea's phone was different to that on Viv's which of course was different to that on mine, so who knows what was going to happen. Viv and me both agreed on one thing though, there's time for another cuppa before leaving for the workshop.

Surprisingly, the rain soon slows then stops. We head out two up on Viv's Honda Hornet avoiding the huge puddles of standing water, open his workshop and get back to work on Solid Air's gearbox and final race preparation. Other little jobs crop up that need attending to, such as loose end plate studs and both the left and right floorboard struts needed welding where the last Teesside crashes had bent and split them. Luckily, the exhaust issue was only down to the (non-working) exhaust gas temperature probe coming loose and so was an easy fix with a spot or two of weld plugging the hole left by the now absent probe. Eventually everything came together, jobs were completed, and we were both happy that the scooter was in as good a condition as possible for the next day's six hours of racing. Not as early as we would have liked maybe, we headed off to the track Viv on his Hornet and me on Solid Air, to meet up with Shane who couldn't leave until the Friday morning due to work. Shane had delays too, not getting away from work promptly and then meeting heavy Friday afternoon traffic on the A1, but amazingly we all arrived at the track within minutes of each other at 5pm and found Andrea already there wondering where we were.

The Autodrome was under a rain cloud when we arrived, and some riders were tentatively riding round the track trying to avoid the treacherous wet areas where the go-karts and drift cars leave half of their tyre rubber behind. This causes problems in certain parts of the course for the scooters, making the racing line very slippery. In the first BSEC endurance race in 2019 many riders fell because of this during a heavy downpour, so we were wary. We decided to fit wet tyres in anticipation of more rain and finally got the scooter out on to the track towards the end of the practice session when, would you believe it, the rain had stopped, and the track was starting to dry out. The track wasn't as slippy as I'd thought it would be and it was good to get a few laps completed, ridding myself of any jitters, so that the following morning we could all get straight out on to the track and concentrate on improving lap times.

The following morning the weather we saw out of the window was not the downpour of rain we were expecting. We didn't have clear skies but at least it wasn't raining. The sun was trying to break through and dry the roads out. Things looked promising but as we all know, what the weather forecast advertises and what actually happens can be two hugely different things so we wait to see what will happen through the day.

At the circuit, most teams are busying around carrying out last minute preparations. Our paddock neighbours and fellow Road Class team are DC10 SERT, with their bright red, old large frame Vespa which they are having problems with. These endurance races have a great atmosphere and camaraderie between the teams with help being offered where possible and despite their gremlins, Stuart Hannay from DC10 SERT still offers cups of tea to us from his Talbot camper van while his more mechanically minded teammates busy away. This also highlights how while it's great having skilled mechanics in the team, it is also useful to have people with other attributes too. Andrea will be our timekeeper and pit board controller, calling riders in as necessary through the day but sadly, we are missing Gary for this race, who freely admits to being of no mechanical use whatsoever but who, along with his wife Jo, is great at keeping the tea and coffee topped up and breakfast rolls supplied from their camper van. To paraphrase a well-known saying about the army, a race team rides on its belly, particularly me.

Qualifying practice takes place, and we change back to dry tyres for this as rain doesn't seem imminent at the moment. The three riders; Shane, Viv, and I, all have good stints out on track and with our best lap time we have a mid-grid start position. I hold Solid Air ready for Shane who is first out on track. This race is being streamed live on YouTube and BSEC's Mike Bonnett is doing a sterling job of carrying out quick trackside interviews with the teams and points out to the viewers how our teams scooter is ridden all year round as well as to this race meeting. Normally, these six hour races would start at 11am on the dot but only two days earlier the nation was hit with the news of the death of Queen Elizabeth II, so today we would be holding a two minute silence in her memory before the race starts. This is respectfully observed and then Keith Terry calls the grid to order by holding a Union Flag aloft on the start line. The engines of all the team's bikes are being noisily revved in anticipation of the drop of the flag. The riders are poised on the opposite side of the track, ready to sprint as agilely as they can in their race leathers and boots to the waiting machines. The tension builds as Keith checks that no one is creeping forward to gain an advantage and then the flag drops. Mayhem ensues as riders dash across the tarmac to take hold of their waiting machines and get as far forward in the race position stakes as they possibly can. The Le Mans start provokes such a mad dash among riders that we have spoken a few times about letting the adrenaline fuelled competition race off to make mistakes in the heat of the moment, while our first rider settles himself down quickly picking off the slower riders as he goes. This is Shane's plan today and it works. He takes the scooter and lets a few riders go in front to avoid contact and is well towards the back of the grid as he rides away. It only takes him a few laps though before he regains his original position and then moves forward, picking off rider by rider until he is in the top ten.

Towards the end of Shane's first leg the rain starts to come down. The decision is now whether to stay on the dry tyres and gamble that the weather improves or change to wet tyres, maybe losing twenty minutes changing them. Shane comes into the pits for a fuel top up and to hand over to me. Discussing the tyre issue with Viv, I had decided to stick with those we have and gauge the conditions as I go rather than give time away. As I ride out Viv is cursing to himself that we should have changed the dry tyres. I'm happy riding in wet conditions, riding smooth normally works well but it will depend on the track itself. I get a few laps under my belt, and everything is okay so continue clocking up the laps. The rain does worsen but there isn't any significant standing water, and I don't feel heavier treaded tyres will make enough difference to warrant stopping to change them. This tactic seems to work, in fact I'm amazed at how well the tyres work in the varying conditions and the track doesn't seem to be as slippery as I had imagined. Confidence is the key, many riders hate being out in the wet so there is advantage to be gained and overtaking is still perfectly possible, providing it is calculated and smooth rather than with the bravado that dry conditions bring out in riders. The laps go by, the rain is continually changing strength, but it does not stop, and the water is finding its way through my gloves and the zip on my leathers to the T-shirt below, but so far so good. I see the pit board calling me in and I hand Solid Air over to be filled up with fuel and tell Viv before he goes out that everything is okay out there, just keep it smooth. And he does just that, clocking up good consistent lap times, speeding up when he can and slowing down when he needs to.

It is still a race despite the weather and people are trying their best to be the fastest they can be in the far from perfect conditions. Shane keeps racking up the laps getting us up to an amazing fifth position overall and leading our group. Everything is working well. Rather than do a refuel as on the previous pit stop between Viv and Shane, I take a calculated chance on just doing a straight rider swap to save a bit of time, but towards the end of the leg I was getting twitchy thinking I'd made the wrong decision and worry about running out of fuel. Andrea puts the pit board out for Shane bringing him in five minutes early just in case, but he misses it a couple of times. I'm getting really panicky by that point and picture him running out of petrol on the back straight, having to push the scooter back and so losing our leading position in the group. He finally comes into the pit, refuels and I get out for the next hour. Conditions were still variable, but I keep it steady and consistent even if my lap times were not my fastest. I'm still getting plenty of overtakes done though, and I am particularly chuffed with the ones on the big sweeping right hander after the straight and we are keeping our group lead too. I have a great tussle with the rider from #207 Valley SC. Their blue small frame Vespa is beautifully prepared and goes like a rocket on the straight, but they have had trouble getting the settings right lower down in the rev range, making it difficult for them in the bendy bits, and that plays into my hand. I'm able to get past him but if I am in front at the start of the straight, I am way behind by the end of it! Talking with Michael Eaves the rider later, he tells me that it was like being on the Star Ship Enterprise from Star Trek when Captain Kirk issues the order "Warp Speed Mr Sulu". With the rain drops heading seemingly horizontal towards his crash helmet visor, he says it feels like riding into fast approaching stars. I finally get some space between us when he gets caught up with a group of riders that I am able to pass quickly and finally break away from him. What an engine though, all 154cc of it!

Towards the end of my stint, some of the other riders are taking some risks in their overtaking and I need to take evasive action two or three times to avoid them hitting me. Not wanting to get caught up with this and crash out, I slow down a touch telling myself to "Just keep it upright" and "I just need to get through the next ten minutes" and, as he tells me later, this gives Viv the heebie-jeebies watching my times drop and he shouts at me to speed up. Because of this, I get called in five minutes earlier than planned. After a refuel and a pat on the back, Viv gets out for the last leg. We have maybe four laps in hand, so he knows all he has to do is rack up some steady and consistent times and not crash, while we just have to hope that there are none of those mechanical gremlins lurking in the shadows to cause any trouble, that's not what we need, or is it?

The commentators for the race livestream had noticed a potential problem that we hadn't seen and wouldn't until we watched the replay later that night. In the race rules, each rider must complete a minimum amount of race time as well as a maximum amount of riding time per stint to ensure teams do not give excessive favour to their quicker riders. The maximum rider time in one go is 65 minutes and Viv went out on to the track with 67 minutes to go! If Viv had rode for 67 minutes and came home as winner in our class, we would be penalised for the rider's excessive time and then "lose" the race. But we are all unaware of this. Viv continues riding and trackside our nerves were becoming increasingly ragged as we watched. We were still leading and still had laps in hand, so everything was good, until 20 minutes from the end.

Shane, Andrea, and I all suddenly notice Viv pull into the pit lane. We look at each other in horror before sprinting round to meet him and find out what has happened. "Broken gear cable!" Viv shouts from inside his crash helmet. We sprint to our paddock area and whip the side panel off, before removing the quick release handlebar top from my home-made race handlebars and performing the quickest cable change in history. A few people are milling round to see what has happened and take photos while team #38 SRP Racetech, across from us in the paddock and in second place behind us in Road Class, understandably cannot believe their luck. The cable is replaced, bodywork refitted and Viv bump starts Solid Air to get back out on track to hopefully regain the lead.

Time passes painfully and slowly. We are constantly scanning the track and checking on Viv's position using the live updates on our phones. Andrea comments, "Where's number 38?". Shane and I don't immediately understand but then we realise, where is #38 SRP Racetech? Who took the group lead because of our broken gear cable? Then from the left, their scooter and rider are slowly trundling along the straight not looking at all happy. No one knows what has happened apart from we have the lead back and it is not long to go till the chequered flag. C'mon Viv, bring it home mate!

Road Class Winners – Team Solid Air
L to R Viv McCann, Andrea McCann,
me and Shane Hunsdale

Quality not quantity!
BSEC Committee Scooter Award

And he does. The biggest smiles are on all of our faces as we meet him in the pits. He holds up a questioning index finger asking "first?" "Yes mate, we won, fantastic, well done!" The feeling is amazing, I am so proud and so happy. Three races this year on my road scooter, all finished and for two of those meetings Solid Air is ridden to the event and then ridden home again too. I joke that I have achieved what I wanted to so now me, and my scooter can retire at the top, but the others unsurprisingly don't agree with me. What a result and on this occasion, those pesky gremlins are not so pesky, someone else's bad luck is our good luck. Apart from the broken gear cable the scooter performed impeccably but even that helped us to come home first, you have got to ride your luck sometimes. We hear that SRP Racetech's rider had been knocked off by another scooter, thankfully he is okay, but that is racing and another day they will get the luck.

We park up Solid Air on the paddock stand where we met Viv and leave it there, just trying to take it all in, winning the Road Class on a true road scooter. I buy a few bottles of celebratory beer for the team, and we soak up a wonderful feeling. As always there is a big crowd when Keith Terry ends the day with a speech and the trophy presentations. Walking up as a team to collect our trophy was like walking on air and we receive a massive cheer from the crowd when they hear that I rode to the event and will ride home again too. Amazingly we then also find out that we finished third in our class over the three races giving us two trophies to take home. But then we really peak when Keith awards the BSEC Committee Scooter Award to Solid Air for its overall achievement at the event. I am dumbstruck, the others push me forward to collect the smallest trophy, it is just about big enough to be used as an egg cup and has got to be my proudest achievement in all my time of riding scooters. Eventually, knackered and after many calls of "well done" and "top job" we head home for a celebratory takeaway, a few drinks and to start watching the race all over again on YouTube.

Over 400 on-road miles, two practice sessions and six hours of full on race time in unsavoury conditions on its own is amazing but to take the class win and finish sixth overall too, is something that will stay with me forever. When I arrive home the following day, I am still amazed at what we had achieved. My girlfriend Kerry wraps me in the biggest hug and wants to hear all about the race, while Solid Air is parked up for the night but gets very little rest, being pulled out of the shed for its usual daily commute to work on Monday morning, followed by a trip back up north for the LCGB Coast to Coast riding event the following weekend. The response that the achievement receives from friends, fellow endurance racers and people on the Team Solid Air and BSEC Facebook pages is phenomenal, but my favourite quote comes from my good friend Nigel Sleightholm of Privateer Racing who simply said… "That's how you do endurance racing!"

Overlooking Morecambe Bay. Heading for the LCGB Coast to Coast one week after the race win

Scooter racing and big smiles at Whilton Mill

AN ITCH THAT NEEDED SCRATCHING?

When Nigel and Paul asked me to join them in Privateer Racing their timing could not have been more perfect. Life was a struggle, my marriage of almost 30 years was coming to an end and would be finished before the first race took place. It was a heartbreaking time but this new venture, along with making a new life for myself, gave me the focus and motivation that would be needed to drag me through some tough times, and along with my children and a few close friends, my Privateer Racing teammates helped to pull me through those times.

After riding for many years on the road, I soon found that whilst a lot of techniques and experiences are transferable on to the track, there are many subtle differences too. As Keith Terry always mentions at a BSEC race brief, DO NOT do the shoulder checks as you do on the road. Look where you are going and use your peripheral vision, let the faster riders go around you, they can and will. Two mantras from my Advanced Motorcycle Training days were "slow in, fast out" (most of the time) using the best line approaching a bend for visibility while being able to stop in the distance that could be seen, and "maximum progress maximum safety". In racing though, as everybody knows, speed is the key and because you are repeatedly riding round the same circuit, without the hazards normally associated with riding on the road (manhole covers and car drivers to name but two), then the line used is for maximum grip and maximum progress. Rather than pelting round at 100% effort though, it is a good idea to keep just a little in reserve, to keep in control of yourself and the bike, rather than becoming a slave to the red mist that racing can induce. It is of no use being the fastest rider out on the track if you cannot finish the race. At well past 50 years of age now, getting out on the track made me realise how much racing was an itch that I had needed to scratch.

PART 5

WE ARE THE ROGUE CREW

SCANDI RAID LAMBRETTA RALLY
Ängelholm 2023
Lambretta
ROGUE CREW

THE SCANDI RAID LAMBRETTA RALLY 2023

A merrily drunken lunch sat outside a friendly Greek restaurant in Libramont during the Belgian Euro Lambretta of 2022, saw Ian Flynn, Paul Slaney and me, ruminating over the following year's Euro Rally home venue and the subsequent lack of an organised overseas trip. The further into the meal we got, the more we were sure that we still wanted a European adventure and so decided that we would stage our own mini Euro rally. Where to go was the next question. Another BLC member with us in Belgium, Andy Neville, was keen for a euro rally return to Scandinavia, so with that idea we had a destination sorted and the Scandi Raid of 2023 was born.

Returning home, Paul set about organising stopovers and campsites and also made contact with German, Danish and Swedish scooter clubs that we could meet up with along the way. Route plans were discussed, and others were invited along for the trip, and after a time we had 25 – 30 people along for the ride. Sadly, over the months some had to drop out due to family or work commitments leaving us with a core group of 18 riders who became known as The Rögue Crew, a disparate bunch of solo and club riders from various areas around the country. Over the following months, we shared thoughts and ideas for the trip over WhatsApp, which also helped to set the tone of humour for the duration, imagine lots of double-entendres style humour as used in the old Carry On… films and you won't be far wrong. Along with the admittedly low level of humour being set, plans and designs for T-shirts, stickers and legshield banners for the trip were made between the group. Allan Tait rose to the challenge here and produced some excellent stickers with Warren Smith producing a brilliant design for the banner. Sadly, and despite his admirable efforts, Allan had to drop out of the trip at short notice but there will be evidence of his input in the depths of Scandinavia for some time to come yet.

Making plans. L to R Me, Ian Flynn and Paul Slaney

Eventually we had a plan. It was decided that everyone would meet as a group in Lübeck, northern Germany, having made their own way from the UK (or Finland as in Paul's case) using whatever route they wanted. From there, Sweden was a relatively short ride through Denmark. What was not planned at this point was venturing further north into Norway to take in a bit more of the Scandinavian scenery and dropping into a local scooter club rally that just happened to be taking place while we were there. With being so close to some spectacular countryside and exquisite riding roads, it would be a shame to have to miss that out.

All that was really left to do was to count down the days to our departure.

Monday 22nd May

Eventually, the time arrived and with different departure dates, routes and channel crossings, everyone started to wind their way across Europe to meet for the first time as a group in Lübeck. I was meeting Steve Watkins, a friend from the Midlands, on the way to the Eurotunnel while Shane Hunsdale, of the Mercenaries SC, Ulster Lambretta Club and co-rider in Team Solid Air, was planning to leave a day later, joining us as we headed across Germany. The two of us made steady progress, leaving France, and heading towards Ghent in Belgium for our first overnight stop. I'd arranged for us to stay in the quirky Treck Indoor Camping hostel, which used old caravans parked up inside a large warehouse for people to stay in, just a short tram ride from the city centre. The hostel had a fun, hippyish, laid back and friendly feel to it and while our caravan may have been rocking it was more to do with the two big, burly scooterboys doing an admirable impression of a couple of tinned sardines rather than any amorous intentions between them!

Just a mile or two before we reached the hostel though, we had our first mechanical incident of the trip. Steve's exhaust supporting brackets had broken and the box pipe was hanging down and scraping along the Belgian tarmac. After some head scratching, we decided to bodge some support for the exhaust using a few twists of lockwire hoping that would get us to the hostel at least. If only. Not even 500 yards down the road the wire had let go, Steve's scooter was sounding like a liberating British tank from World War II and the exhaust lay forlornly on the road behind us. The exhaust was retrieved, strapped to the rest of Steve's luggage and we made our way to the hostel while locals covered their ears and protected small children from the din as we rode along. Once settled into the night's accommodation we then headed off to the Dulle Griet bar in the city centre and its vast array of Belgian beers, whilst putting out a call for help on social media and to various contacts for assistance. This is where modern technology and the Lambretta family really came into its own. The Lambretta Club Belgium were fantastic with various offers of help being made, including an offer of a complete replacement from a British expat living just outside Ghent. Messages were exchanged and plans made to meet at his house the following morning, so we made the most of the delights of the Dulle Griet, before heading back to our caravan and a restful sleep.

Tuesday 23rd May

Having bought a Lambretta LD125 early this year and joining the Lambretta Shaft Riders Page on Facebook, I was already familiar with the name Terence Newman, and now Steve and I found ourselves riding to his house to take up his kind offer of a replacement AF Clubman exhaust to help us on our way. We were greeted by a charming, and very youthful, 82-year-old gentleman who hadn't developed an interest in the Lambretta scooter until he was a spritely 62, seven years older than I was when we met, but he is certainly making up for lost time. We chatted, were shown his collection of characterful scooters, and introduced to his lovely wife Sonja, who provided us with coffee and pastries and let me feed her chickens. Eventually, attention was given to the job in hand, but rather than swap exhausts it was decided, once Terry told us that he could weld, that it would be better to weld the exhaust brackets back onto the box rather than replace the whole exhaust, then Steve could buy a new exhaust along the way as a back up replacement. Despite Terry's humble claims he was "shit at welding," he said he would do what he could. He busied away, preparing the metalwork, and setting up his tools while looking in his absolute element. With his music blaring away in the outbuilding and continual conversation between the three of us, the job was soon done, and the necessary adjustments made to line the exhaust up on the scooter. Once the repair was complete, we gave our thanks and said our farewells to Terry and Sonja to then set off in the direction of Scooter Centre Köln (SCK) and the chance to buy a new exhaust.

With a delightful gentleman in Belgium. L to R Steve Watkins, Terence Newman and me

Belgium roads tend to fall into two types, aside from the motorways. One is nicely rural and quiet whilst the other seems to be never ending urbanity. Not big city urban, just relentlessly built up, where one village melds into another, filling in the gaps between built up areas, not allowing us time to open the throttle and wind our scooters up a bit. It makes the riding slow and tedious and sadly this is what we experienced for a good couple of hours after leaving Terry. Eventually, we resorted to jumping on the motorway to make up for lost time and headed into Germany for a campsite about 30 minutes south of SCK. The camping area was right next to a scenic lake of crystal clear water. "I fancy a swim" I said to Steve, who, when I got changed into my shorts, exclaimed "Bloody hell! I thought you were kidding!" Steve doesn't share the same enthusiasm for freshwater swimming, "There's fish and stuff in there!" he protested, as I floundered around and enjoyed myself, taking care not to be eaten alive by the resident minnows.

Wednesday 24th May

A tasty meal of paprika schnitzel, and rosti potatoes along with a few Kölsch beers in a local bar the previous night, where the waitress ensured our glasses were never empty and the average age of fellow drinkers seemed to be at least 84, set us up for today's ride to SCK and then further north into Germany. I'm sure the vast majority of British scooterists know of SCK and their BGM branded parts, and even without the failure of Steve's exhaust we had decided to take a detour and visit the shop. Whilst it's not a shop in the traditional sense of the word since they restructured the whole set-up, it is well worth a visit. Situated in an industrial area, walking into the showroom is not far short of breathtaking. The sparse and modern showroom, in classic white décor, houses around 50 Vespas and Lambrettas. Ranging from a Vespa so rusty it's amazing that it holds itself together, to an old style Lambretta kneeler sprinter, onto a gaggle of PK range Vespas, Luna line Lambrettas, custom machines and the totally gorgeous BGM Lambretta GP demonstrator, which I first set eyes on at the Adria Euro Lambretta in 2017, oh and the first of quite a few immaculate and rare Vespa SS90s contained within the building. On this occasion, jaw dropping is an appropriate description, especially when you realise that all the machines on display and contained within the building are owned by just one person.

Just wow! Scooter Centre Köln

An immaculate Vespa SS90 on display

Rather than approaching the shop counter with a grubby paper list in your mitts, there are several touchscreens set on top of stylish picnic style tables with benches where you can sit and peruse the offerings available at your leisure. The warehouse staff will then select the parts and bring your dreams to you. Steve positioned himself at one of these benches to order the required exhaust, along with a few other items requested by others in the Rögue Crew, but after numerous attempts to navigate both modern technology and a language barrier, he called in the cavalry, in the form of Maryza, who provided able assistance to complete the purchase.

Maryza then offered to take us on a guided tour of the SCK business; including the showroom, warehouse, offices, and the unique rooftop scooter storage area. The business is huge and nothing like anything scooter related I know of in the UK. It could be a warehouse for any type of business, but when you read the box labels as you wander round the heart can miss a beat as you realise that all the goodies contained within could keep your own little workshop stocked for a long, long time. The staff are all friendly and we are led out of the warehouse, up some stairs, through offices and into the boardroom. All the way along, the thing that astounded both Steve and me are the many scooters scattered around. In stairwells, corridors and kitchens there are collectable machines in original or immaculate condition. Vespa Rallys, Spanish Lambrettas, brand new PXs, Lambretta Lis, SXs and more genuine SS90s than I ever thought was possible to have in one place. Phillip, the boss, welcomes us into his office and there sat unassumingly in the corner is a gorgeous red and white Lambretta, as if everybody has one in their office!

Finally, Steve collects his exhaust, we say goodbye and proffer our thanks to Maryza, who takes our photos in front of the showroom and wishes us well on our journey. Overwhelmed by the sights we have just seen, I go straight onto autopilot, and ride onto the correct left side of the road for riding at home until I hear Steve hollering at the top of his voice warning me of my imminent doom and the fact that we are riding in Germany... on the right!

Having survived that incident, we have a nice straight forward ride for the rest of the day and head to a campsite near Cloppenberg, just north of Osnabrück, where we should be meeting Ian, Andy and hopefully Shane. Meeting Ian and Andy is straight forward enough. We get to the prearranged campsite to find it's a bit of a ghost town, and like a lot of campsites in Germany, it's more of a retreat for static caravan owners who visit week after week but maybe only live a short drive away. With no prospect of any food or drink, we do a quick recce of a couple of other nearby sites and message the Bristol boys with details of where we're going to spend the night. Not much later they arrive, camp is quickly set, and we head off into the nearby town of Garrel for pizzas, kebabs, and a few cans to drink around the tent. Shane on the other hand is not quite so straight forward.

Thursday 25th May

In the build up to departure, Shane had attempted plans A, B and C of different engine set-ups for the trip before finally settling on an RT195, which he finished building on the day he should have been crossing into mainland Europe. After who knows how many hours of spannering, he eventually set off to catch an evening ferry and ended up riding through the night, arriving at our campsite at 10am the following morning. This was both a feat of stamina and an episode of sheer lunacy, which I'm convinced he was only capable of doing as he earns his living driving lorries through the night, it is still impressive though. When we arrived, he looked dazed but with a hot drink inside him he soon livened up so that we could all set off together bound for Lübeck, just north of Hamburg, to meet up with the rest of the Rögue Crew, but not before dropping into see Christian Albrecht at his Salem Speed workshop just outside the city.

Paul had contacted Christian, along with other Lambretta clubs along the route, in anticipation of meeting up with them along the way. The idea of stopping off at a workshop was genius, giving people a chance to adjust or to fix their scooter, while also having parts and aid on hand if needed.

Earlier along the route we had bumped into Warren Smith and Richard Khybett of the Gremlins SC and at Salem Speed we caught up with father and son duo Keith and Dan Reynolds, before meeting up later that evening with the Manchester Lyons group and Paul Slaney. It was great to get everyone together properly for the first time, catch up and share tales of the journey so far. The evening got even better when we were told that the Lübeck Lambretta Club had arranged a meet up at a local bar with its own brewery and a very tasty line in pizzas, just a short taxi ride away. The night was a great success, and we received a warm reception from the locals. Of course, when we returned to the hotel a few more drinks were sunk, except for one person that it is. After his epic ride the night before, poor old Shane had nodded off propped up between a couple of other Rögue Crew members. So, like a kid who had fallen asleep under the table at a party and who had to be woken up by a parent, he was stirred awake and told to go to bed, while we carried on drinking.

The Lübeck Lambretta Club

Friday 26th May

18 scooters leave the hotel in the morning but split into the smaller groups that they arrived in to make progress easier. The plan is to catch the Puttgarden to Rødby ferry for a day's ride through Denmark up to Copenhagen, but there are problems when we reach the ferry terminal. There are queues leading up to all the check-in barriers. The whole computer network for the ferry company had crashed causing chaos. The ferries cross every 30 minutes so there won't be a major delay if the planned ferry is missed, but there are still many irate and impatient travellers delayed on the wrong side of the barriers, particularly when I amble up to the kiosk and have a chat with the very helpful chap there as I have misplaced my email booking confirmation, causing some waiting female German or Danish travellers to get just a touch upset with me. They were not happy at all, but I escaped unharmed, just. Slowly cars, bikes and scooters were let through the barriers to join the queue to board the next ferry, which meant some of our group caught one ferry and then had to wait on the other side while the rest of the group caught another.

The ride through Denmark was very non-descript. The roads were quiet, a lot of them were straight and boring with a strong crosswind that took the enjoyment out of the ride for a lot of the group. Eventually we arrive at Peter's Garage, just outside Copenhagen, and the only scooter workshop in Denmark. Again, a small group of local scooterists made the effort to come and meet us and it was great to chat and see how things are different for them compared to back home. The big similarity with everyone that we meet along the way is the passion and enthusiasm for the humble scooters that we all ride, whether it's just locally or over long distances as we were on this trip. Peter was very welcoming and the first thing he did was to point everyone in the direction of the fridge for a cold drink on our arrival. When we arrived, there was already a Rögue scooter up on a ramp having attention to its front brake and immediately Shane started work on what he thought was a slipping clutch that turned out to be a kickstart mechanism issue. The problem was solved with enthusiastic, smiling assistance from Peter, which bearing in mind that he was making a mammoth trip down to the SIP Scootershop in Germany on his Egig engined Vespa small frame, was beyond anything we expected.

On leaving the workshop, we were accompanied by one of Peter's friends on his very quick Vespa small frame. He would shoot past the group, stop up ahead and take some pictures or speed past us, whilst riding one handed, taking a video of us all on his phone. I was riding at the back of the group and had briefly noticed a twin head lighted motorcycle hanging back in the distance behind us. The next thing I knew, a motorcycle police officer glided past us with a signal to the Danish Vespa rider indicating in no uncertain terms that he should pull over and stop, now! Sadly, for him a 2000 Danish Krone (over £200) fine was handed out while we had to ride past and continue our ride. We were all camping on the outskirts of Copenhagen but sadly were unable to explore the sites of the capital city, instead making do with some food and drink from a local supermarket and another campsite chat into the chilly night before heading into Sweden the following morning.

Saturday 27th May

Sitting at the back of the group and watching our cluster of scooters ride up and over the almost 10 mile long Øresund Bridge connecting Denmark and Sweden, was a complete buzz, especially as it announced our entry in Sweden. It is an amazing feat of engineering and somewhere I had wanted to ride for a while, and I wasn't disappointed. The group was swiftly moved on by a friendly but very firm border security guard when we stopped to regroup at a point where we should not have, so as instructed, we moved half a mile up the road to the official rest point. As we all pulled into park, we were followed in by a group of bikers with a very impressive and mixed group of machines. The two groups mingled and discussed destinations, they were impressed with our journey, and we felt we just had to pop into where they were going, the Hepcat Vintage Store open day.

Shortly after we pulled into a petrol station where a welcoming party from the Lambretta Club Malmö were waiting expectantly for us. Our wonderful Swedish hosts had arranged to keep us occupied over the weekend. They had planned a scenic route to our campsite at Ängelholm, a stop off at an American style Road Diner, factored in picking up some alcohol at the state-run off-licences (the Systembolaget), which are only open within certain times each day, and worked out a scenic ride out on the Sunday of some 100 miles, stopping off for a lunch of traditional

Swedish meatballs along the way. Also, when we asked if it was possible to squeeze in a detour to the Hepcat Store, they put their heads together and quickly worked out a reroute, top people indeed!

The Lambretta Club Malmö

We all rolled into the small Swedish town of Lund, and turned our scooters into the area where the Hepcat store was holding its open day. Whatever the crowd that had turned up for the event were expecting, it was not a rag-tag group of fully loaded scooters from the UK and their Swedish counterparts. The two-stroke engine noise of all the scooters and the accompanying cloud of fug stopped EVERYONE in their tracks. Jaws were dropped, cameras clicked, and phones were quickly switched on to video mode to record our entrance. We had arrived in Sweden good and proper.

The Hepcat open day is an annual event attracting Scandinavian hipsters, bikers, vintage muscle cars and hot rods. The Swedes share a real affinity with the American style of the 1950s, 60s and 70s, and it was not unusual to see old American vehicles on the roads throughout our time in Sweden. With all the scooters parked up we mingled with the crowd, admiring all the other vehicles and the locals mingled with us, asking where we were from and where we were going. After 20 minutes or so, we regrouped and started our scooters to leave. Again, everyone stopped to soak up the sight of our group and to wave us off to our destination. The visit really was worth the detour and made one of many lasting memories of the trip.

When we arrived at the campsite later that afternoon, we had much the same effect on the local campers. Our group arrived slightly later due to a snapped gear cable, but we still caught everyone's eye as we rode through to our pitches. The evening was spent on site, at their bar and eating pizza from the restaurant, which strangely seems to be a staple part of the Scandinavian diet. We all noted that the local mozzies were at least twice the size of those at home and they were hungry. The bar closed earlier than we hoped but not hearing a last orders bell or the traditional English call of "Ain't you got homes to got to!", we carried on drinking and the bar staff waited politely as we ordered first, then second, then third last orders before we finally let them lock up and head off home. This air of politeness was repeated out on the roads too. It was not unusual for Swedish drivers to see our group and stop to let us through a junction, often as they were halfway through a roundabout, and people in towns and villages often gave us waves and smiles as we rode through.

Sunday 28th May

Sunday was spent being led through some wonderful riding roads by our hosts from Malmö. The main roads were not particularly busy and when we turned off them into the smaller rural roads, they hardly seemed to be used at all. The roads were smooth and full of curves, through pretty countryside, with lots of horses in fields that would startle as we approached and then do a few circuits of their paddocks until we had passed by. They obviously were not used to the sight and sound of a group of scooters passing their fields. We stopped at one point for someone's broken clutch cable to be replaced, and all that could be heard was the wind in the trees and the song of birds, not even any traffic in the distance to disturb the peace, lovely. A few people stayed at the campsite to carry out repairs on their scooter or just needing a day out of the saddle, but those that went all agreed it was well worth the ride to get off the beaten track and see rural Sweden.

Monday 29th May

This was the day most of the group headed back to the UK catching a ferry from Trelleborg back to Lübeck and Paul set off back towards Finland, while I had decided to tag along with Shane who was heading into Norway before visiting the Restless SC at their club rally, the Classic Scooter Run 23 in Oslo. The plan was to head further north into Sweden then cross into Norway. Having said our goodbyes, it wasn't long before the scooter gremlins that had been plaguing Shane so far on the trip made an unwelcome return. His HT cap started bouncing off the spark plug whenever he hit a bump in the road causing the engine to die and so a replacement was fitted, then not much further on a gear cable snapped resulting in a colourful mix of Gaelic and old English words to be heard coming from Shane's mouth. This happened just half a mile from the motorway exit we were taking, so keeping one eye on the carriageway and the traffic coming towards us we busied about fitting a fresh cable.

Shane replacing a broken gear cable

Swedish roads in the areas we visited seem to be either small bendy country roads or long and quite straight ones, the equivalent of A-Roads back home but with a lot less traffic. The scenery is very pleasant, lots of trees and occasional lakes which become more frequent the further north you go. Whilst the roads are not overly exciting, they do make for good progress and the miles can be racked up at a steady speed. We kept an eye on fuel use just in case petrol stations became scarce, but that was a concern that we didn't need to worry about. It's not unusual for the filling stations to be just a couple of pumps (Diesel and E10) with a card payment point but no shop or toilets. We clocked up about 200 miles that day, ending up at a lake side campsite with a restaurant attached to provide us with more pizza and expensive beer.

Tuesday 30th May

The next day was much of the same, just making our way north. We were following one road, the E26 and thinking that would be straight forward enough I switched off my phone satnav to save some data. How wrong I was. We realised that the Swedish direction signs don't always carry the road numbers like at home, so following a road having not seen a sign labelled with E26 directing us elsewhere, we would stop to check if we were heading in the right direction only to find that we should have turned off at a junction some miles back. After this happening a couple of times we returned to using my phone for directions, with instructions sent through the headset. Two things were noticed today, one was most cars having three or four high powered spotlights fitted to the front of their cars, presumably so the resident moose could see them coming (they are a LOT bigger than the deer at home) and the other was the amount of people that talked to us along the way that owned Lambrettas. They were all amazed at our trip and after a friendly chat would wish us a safe journey.

We were close to reaching the day's destination of Alvdalens with no mechanical trouble for Shane when I noticed something hanging underneath his scooter and scraping the tarmac as we rode along. Quickly nipping in front and pulling him over, we found the tailpipe of his Pro Clubman exhaust had ditched its supporting bracket and loosened off the securing nuts. We decided to remove the tailpipe and performing some bodgery at the campsite, which we did with a control cable, a nut, bolt, and a couple of big washers. The campsite was next to a wide river that was running really high and fast with very cold melted snow water coming down from the mountains. As we set our tents up, we realised that the loud buzzing we could hear was not from an oversized mosquito but a teenage Swedish lad on his little automatic moped, riding round the campsite blipping the throttle and looking for his mates. Wandering around the local town shortly after, we were surprised by the variety of modified Volvos that were slammed, adorned with wide wheels and garish stickers, or blaring out loud music. It is good to see some things are the same wherever you go just with a different make of vehicle and taste in music.

Wednesday 31st May

A 70 mile ride to Idre on quiet Swedish roads was made difficult by a strong and constant head wind. The traffic is sparse, and the roads are long and straight, so it is possible to stop and take photos with my scooter parked in the middle of the road in relative safety. There are many more lakes in the area and deforested areas that resemble a decimated World War One landscape with just the occasional tree stump left behind.

The traffic in Sweden was horrendous!

Another border crossed, with Shane Hunsdale

As we get closer to the Norwegian border, there is still snow left on the ground and we can see snow topped mountains in the distance. The road taking us across the border is the equivalent of a UK B-Road, with just an old stack of boulders set back from the road marking the change that is topped with a sign reading "Sverige" on one side and "Norge" on the other, and another more modern border sign next to the road, which we duly adorn with a Rögue Crew sticker and take the obligatory selfie in front of.

The scenery changes straight away, becoming much more dramatic, colder and the wind is even stronger. The roads in this area are not as well maintained and gravelled roads are not unusual. We ride down to a lakeside village called Elgå, stopping to allow a small group of reindeer to move out of the road. The biggest male does not look at all perturbed by our presence, giving us his best stare, before they all slip into the woodland

and quickly disappear. Down at the lakeside, the wind was blowing a right old hooley and as much as I like a freshwater swim, there was no way I was going to risk hypothermia for a quick dip here. As we ride on, the landscape becomes strewn with large boulders, the road surface quality is variable, and the wind doesn't let up. We pass a very welcoming roadside restaurant in a town called Os and decide we need some sustenance and warmth. The waiter tries to convince him that their plate sizes are very generous, but the slightly built Shane is insistent that he wanted a burger, some chips, AND a kebab. The waiter was left impressed.

On the edge of Lake Femunden at Elgå

Leaving the restaurant, we experience a short but sharp rain shower, amazingly the only rain of the whole trip, and as we ride towards the campsite the light from the setting sun shining through the rain clouds with the mountains in the background is quite breath taking. Booking into the campsite as Shane refuels, I take advantage of a very reasonably priced spare chalet rather than pitching the tents, and we both appreciate the warmth from it's radiators as the temperature plummets. Making use of the extra hours of daylight that Norway gets, Shane tinkers with his scooter and adjusts the carb on his first fully trouble free day of the trip so far.

Thursday 1st June

Chatting the night before, we had considered taking a detour north to Trondheim and the fjords there. However, waking up to the still low temperatures and what would be a head wind for the 100 or so miles to reach it, and being reminded of the demanding ride of the day before, we decided to stick to our original plan and head for Lillehammer. In the months leading up to this trip Shane and I had been talking about riding up to Nordkapp on the furthest north tarmacked road within the arctic circle, but this trip has helped us realise just how big an expedition that would be having spoken to people along the way, taking into account the huge distances involved and how severe the weather can be that far north. Even in what would be the height of summer back home, the journey would be a massive challenge just to say we had been there and makes me feel a rethink might be needed for that trip.

So, Lillehammer it was. After some kickstart issues on Shane's scooter delaying the start slightly, we rode out of Tynset and within five minutes were following an almost deserted road south towards Koppang. This road was a delight to ride with its silky smooth surface following a sweeping route that was bordered by hills, forest, rivers and mountains. Oncoming cars were rare, and we only met one other going in our direction, which we quickly overtook and left behind. Our route took us over a small single-track girder bridge crossing the river Renaelva, from where we intended heading across country on small woodland roads. The road we had chosen was nothing more than a gravel track though. We followed it for a mile or so but were stopped by a barrier across the road and a sign explaining that repairs were being carried out on a bridge. While we were deciding what to do a pack of kennelled huskies saw us and were kicking up a right old racket, baying at our presence until we left. Following our new route took us along a main road with nothing particular of interest until rounding a bend, I was stunned to see a huge metal moose stood standing by the side of the road. I signalled to pull over, waving frantically at the statue, until Shane eventually noticed what is called Storelgen, or Big Elk or Moose (depending on who you are talking to). Standing at just over 10 metres tall and made of polished stainless steel, it is nothing short of awe inspiring and dwarfed both us and our scooters. It was constructed

Storelgen, he's a BIG fella!

Fairytale church at Sollia

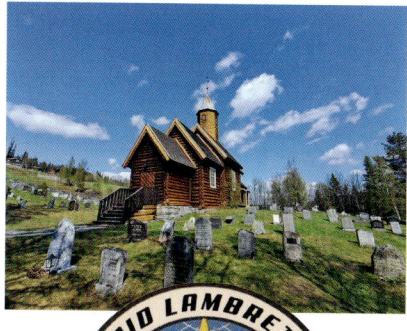

High up in the Rondane National Park

to encourage people to take a break from driving and to warn them of the dangers of these wild animals in the road, and it certainly gets people's attention.

Continuing along, we followed the detour as the roads climbed higher into the hills. We stopped at an old wooden church and wandered around its graveyard. Built in 1738, it looked like something straight out of Hansel and Gretel. Looking down into the valley and off to the distant mountains with beautifully clean air and blue skies, I felt this was as peaceful a final resting place as anyone could wish for.

Further along, we rode into the Rondane National Park. The scenery was much more open, bleak and barren. There was still a lot of snow on the ground and some of the small lakes were frozen. Amazingly there are quite a lot of buildings that look to be permanently inhabited, which considering the harsh conditions, is quite amazing. Further along we ride through what appears to be a winter sport resort. These Norwegians must be a tough bunch. From here the road descends for miles, following a lovely twisty route until finally levelling out and following the river towards our destination of Lillehammer.

SCANDI RAID MAP

1. SALEM SPEED
2. PETER'S GARAGE
3. ØRESUND BRIDGE
4. HEPCAT STORE
5. STORELGEN
6. SOLLIA CHURCH
7. OLYMPIC PARK
8. SCOOTER RUN

SWEDEN

ALVDALENS

TYNSET

OSLO

NORWAY

POLAND
GERMANY
DENMARK
HOLLAND
BELGIUM
FRANCE
BLIGHTY
GHENT
KIEL
LÜBECK
MALMÖ
ANGELHOLM
GOTHENBERG
HEPCAT
N
1
2
3
4

Friday 2nd June

Before we left Lillehammer for Oslo, Shane wanted to show me the ski jumps at the Olympic Park overlooking the town. Anyone who is brave enough to stand at the top of one of those jumps before hurling themselves down the steep narrow strips of ice and snow which launch the skier through the air to hopefully land upright in front of thousands of spectators, risking broken bones and humiliation, deserves an Olympic medal.

Compared to the roads and scenery that we had seen so far, the ride to Oslo was quite uneventful and normal. On the outskirts the traffic built up, there were miles of roadworks to be negotiated and the entire population seemed to be out on the road. Eventually though, we arrived at the Classic Scooter Run 23 and a received a warm welcome on the gate. The venue brought a gasp from us both when we saw the view from the site. The camping area was only small but looked down and over the capital city and its fjords, towards an amazing view which was made even more dramatic by the sight of a solid stone amphitheatre that had been built to take advantage of its location.

Setting up our tents took ages as people were wandering over to say hello and ask about our journey. Both of our scooters were admired by people who came over to chat and Solid Air received loads of positive comments for its patina. "Patina? Battered more like!" I would reply, having only a month earlier completed the BSEC 8 Hour Endurance Race at Whilton Mill, where Shane crashed it and smashed the handlebars. The atmosphere was friendly and relaxed, we made many new friends, including quite a few British expats and some of the Solent Cougars SC who had flown over for the rally. The mix of scooters, people and styles were varied, with Vespas in the majority and in the evening a Norwegian band called The Men entertained the crowd with an energetic set of 1960s mod and garage influenced tunes. The night was bitterly cold but that did not stop a hardy bunch from dancing well into the early hours of the morning.

Saturday 3rd June

We enjoyed a relaxing morning and breakfast was laid on for everyone. Most people mingled and chatted while they waited for the ride out to start. Shane and I both felt that a day of rest was needed so watched as the 200 or so scooters set off to make their way through the outskirts of Oslo while we headed back to give the scooters a check over in preparation for the next day's homeward ride.

Once the ride out had returned to camp, the onsite events got started. A rolling road dyno session gave people the opportunity to check their machine's power output against others, attendees could choose their favourite scooter for the all-included custom show and some hardy riders chose to thrash their scooter around a short grass circuit that had plenty of hidden bumps and a very steep downhill section, catching quite a few riders out and providing spectators with a few spectacular crashes, but thankfully no serious injuries. The temperature dropped harshly when the sun was obscured by cloud, but thankfully the weather in the evening was much warmer than the previous chilly night. Perry Dear and the Deerstalkers kicked off the night's musical entertainment with a definite Merseybeat and sixties instrumental guitar vibe, wearing matching suits and winklepickers. The mainly Norwegian crowd were then treated to an impromptu set from Øystein Greni, the frontman of a celebrated Norwegian rock band called Bigbang. This seemed to be quite a treat for the crowd with him being a former member of the Restless SC, and I must say that hearing him from a distance I did wander over to get a closer listen and was impressed with the blues-tinged sound that I heard.

The organisers had really put a lot of work into organising this club rally and it certainly paid off with a great atmosphere, friendly people, and cracking entertainment. I really enjoyed the DJs who provided a raft of the usual scooter rally sounds, but also threw in a lot of variety too, and I couldn't believe it when I heard for the first time on a rally, a song from one of my all-time favourite bands The Screaming Blue Messiahs, who are not a typical scooter rally sound back home in the UK. As is often the case at a rally, prizes were handed out for awards such as Best Scooter and Dyno Challenge Winner. These winners were asked to place their scooters in front of the stage for the evening and Shane and I were also asked to bring our scooters along as we were to be awarded with the Longest Ride Award, having ridden 2,200 miles just to reach the rally. To say we were chuffed was an understatement.

The Longest Ride Award goes to him and me

Solid Air and Shane's scooter on stage with Los Plantronics

Headlining the evening's entertainment were Los Plantronics, who were described as a "Mariachi Death Surf" band, and what a band they were. They had a frenetic energy for the entire set. The band were dressed up in black Mexican Mariachi outfits trimmed with embroidery and topped with wide brimmed hats while playing loud, fuzzed up garage rock and the front man, who sang, growled and played drums standing up, had the look and energy of a shirtless tattooed Iggy Pop crossed with the masked 1970s wrestler Kendo Nagasaki, imagine that if you can. The set was great, the crowd lapped up the drama and energy of the band and the night was finished off with an almost improbable onstage tyre burnout from a mighty Vespa PX80. What a night!

Sunday 4th June

It was time to head home. Leaving the rally, we were given a lovely send off, receiving lots of waves and farewells. It was quite emotional really and I almost went all soppy and shed a tear, almost. The plan was to jump on the motorway towards Gothenburg then board an overnight ferry to Kiel in Germany. The riding was easy and both scooters were running nicely. After about an hour Shane pulled off the main carriageway to fill up with petrol when his engine revs immediately shot up, screaming like a banshee, grabbing the attention of everyone on the forecourt. Whipping the side panel and air filter off the scooter, I place my hand over the open carburettor starving the engine of oxygen until it came to a stop. A quick postmortem followed but we knew what we were looking for. The high engine revs were caused by too much air getting into the engine through a gap and we found the internal locating lip of the rubber carb mount was torn, allowing the extra air in. Sadly, the one spare part that Shane had left home without was a carburettor rubber mount, so our bodging skills were called into action again. We cut up a rubber glove to wrap around the carb body mount as a sealing tape. Prodding the scooter into life with the kickstart had the desired effect and the engine revved nicely and behaved as it should, success!

On we rode, fingers crossed, towards Gothenburg. Then, after about 10 miles Shane's engine suddenly lost power and we pulled over onto the hard shoulder. The reading on an engine temperature sensor had shot up just before the engine died, not good news. We checked that the carb was still positioned correctly, which it was, and then removed the spark plug which did not look at all healthy. The plug electrode should at least be a nice chocolate brown colour, or darker, showing that the petrol, air, and heat balance is all working well. This plug had a noticeably light grey colour splattered with tiny white dots though, indicating an ominous build up of heat. We both looked at each other knowing what this probably

Los Plantronics on stage   A familiar pose, Shane "Paneloff" Hunsdale

meant. "Put the plug back in and check the compression" I said to Shane, but this only confirmed what we were both dreading. Shane easily pushed the kickstart downwards with his hand, meaning that a massive heat build up (caused by an air leak?) had melted a hole in the piston crown. This was terminal and one bodge too far. With no other choice, Shane called in the cavalry using his European Breakdown Recovery Service. Once it was confirmed that someone would be with Shane soon, I said goodbye and set off on my own, bound for the ferry.

Monday 5th June

I had reached the ferry easily enough the previous day and enjoyed a hot shower in my cabin, some cold beers, a delicious meal, and a good night's sleep. Sadly, Shane had not had such an easy time. The breakdown company was quibbling over recovery costs and had driven Shane to a hotel (at his own expense) while they decided if they were going to recover his scooter or not. As is often the way, money was the issue. The recovery service has a budget to recover a vehicle, if this cost is too high (as it was due to the distance involved in this case) or if the vehicle is not considered valuable enough (this is where an agreed value insurance policy has its use), then there are complications and Shane experienced them fully with this breakdown. After much toing and froing between Shane and the breakdown company, as well as messages back and forth between The Rögue Crew, Shane arranged to fly home (again at his own cost) while some fantastic Norwegians were contacted who agreed to pick his scooter up and look after it until Shane could return and collect it using the remaining recovery budget to pay for ferry crossings and van hire.

In the meantime, I had a lot of miles to cover to get home to return to work on Thursday. I had a Eurotunnel crossing booked for Wednesday but decided to crack on and see if I could get home a day early, leaving me with a day free to adjust to the pending return to normality. I got stuck into racking up the miles with stints of between 65 and 90 miles at a time. The only way to do this was on the motorway sadly, but that is what they were designed for so on I went. I had decided to cruise slower than normal to save on fuel and oil and sat at around 55mph most of the way. The riding was straight forward enough with lorries not allowed to overtake a lot of the time, being forced to stay in lane one mostly. This made things easier for me and I just needed to be aware of extremely fast traffic coming from behind when I was planning an overtake. The only hairy moment of the day occurred when I had just accelerated to overtake a few lorries, and at the same time something caused them to slow down suddenly. I took a sharp intake of breath as the gap between my scooter and the closest lorry dramatically reduced, but thankfully I still had enough time to change position safely and move lanes, just.

Early in the ride I adopted a strategy of ride, stop, refuel, drink, snack, toilet, go. Which, along with my invention of scooter yoga, where one by one I had a quick stretch of my hands, legs, back and shoulders every 10 - 15 miles, passed the time surprisingly easily and I arrived at my overnight stop that evening near Oud-Turnhout in Belgium, some 400 miles later and feeling relatively free of aches and pains.

Tuesday 6th June

A sound night's sleep at a quiet camp site followed by a quick redo of the lockwire that had been securing Solid Air's tailpipe since I left the UK, then packing away my tent for the last time on this trip, saw me eager to get started on the 160 miles to the Eurotunnel. Again, I used the speedier option of the motorway, which took me through miles of traffic and roadworks around Antwerp and Ghent, not fun but necessary.

Don't leave home without lock wire and duct tape

Approaching Calais, the wind strength increased as it always seems to when heading in that direction. Despite that, I arrived in good time to catch an earlier crossing and chatted with bikers heading home from their European trips. I like the ease and speed of this crossing and from Folkestone it is only about 130 miles to get me home. That is if I do not get distracted by a moment of brain fade and head onto the M26, which takes me in completely the wrong direction and then gets me caught up in the miles of traffic that has snarled up due to a lorry fire on the M20. I still do not know why I took that wrong turn as I have taken that route many times over the years. Oh well, I was nearly home, if a bit later than I was hoping. The Dartford Crossing and M25 are predictably busy, making the ride a chore, but eventually I'm within touching distance of home. A quick stop off to pick up a couple of celebratory beers and a freshly fried bag of chips signal the trip to be as good as finished and within 15 minutes I am turning Solid Air's engine off for the last time of this adventure, having completed over 3,100 miles in 16 days. When Kerry gets home, she gives me the biggest and most welcoming hug. I can finally relax.

I always love getting home after a trip, however good it has been, and this time is no different. There is so much to process and log away in my memory bank that it will be some time before I touch down properly. I was finally home though, and all that left me to do was to start planning for my next European adventure.

THE RÖGUE CREW

Along for the ride were… Andrew Burkey, Andy Neville, Dan Reynolds, Gareth Middleton, Gary Stones, Ian Flynn, Keith Reynolds, Kev Johnson, Lee Maddocks, Paul Slaney, Paul Woods, Seamus Murphy, Shane Hunsdale, Richard Khybett, Steve Bell, Steve Watkins and Warren Smith

PART 6

THE FUTURE IS UNWRITTEN

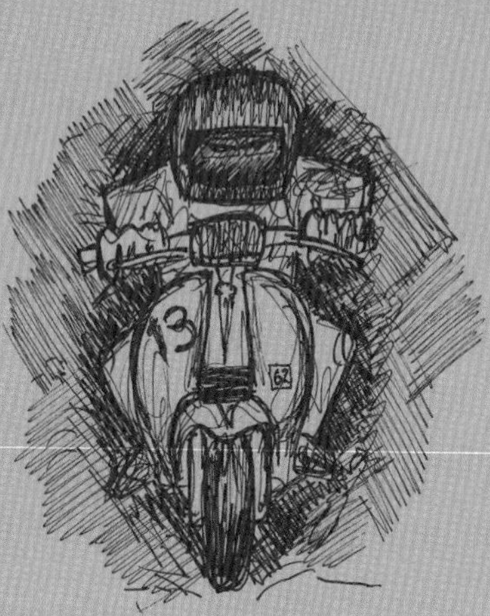

This book is very much about the past, from when I was a kid, but also brings us right up to the present day. It is about memories and what was done to make them. I am not unique, there are many people who could tell similar stories to mine (and more) in the scootering world. I am not claiming to have done the most or ridden the furthest, I have just done what I have done, having a bloody good time along the way and then decided to put it all down in writing after Kerry asked me one day if I had ever thought about writing a book. I fobbed her off at the time.

I have written pieces for the New Jetset (the LCGB members magazine), an article for Scooternova Magazine, as well as reporting on some of my trips on the LCGB Forum and Facebook. Having enjoyed writing about my trips and receiving positive comments about these articles, and after thinking about Kerry's suggestion of writing a book, the question I asked myself was "Why not?" and then "What's to lose?" To which the answer was, as is often the case in life, not a lot. I decided to make a start and see where it went, even if it was just to put something down in writing for my kids and Kerry to see what it is that I get up to when I head out on my scooter. So, I have put some memories into words, and having put those words onto a page I hope that this book will entertain whether the reader is a scooter rider or not, and maybe even inspire others to do something similar on a scooter for themselves.

The scooters we ride do not need to be trendy or cool for us to like them, they are inanimate objects that we inject life into and because of that and how we do it, they have become engrained in British culture. Park a classic scooter, whether rusty and scarred or beautifully restored, next to a Ferrari and it will attract as much, if not more attention, than the bright red Italian motorcar. Maybe because of the memories that they rekindle in the onlooker's mind, the sense of freedom they can induce or just because they are far more easily attainable as a classic vehicle, even if prices have gradually risen due to their popularity during the past decade or so.

Over the years I have met a wide variety of interesting and entertaining people through riding a scooter. Some people became long term friends while others came and went. Looking back at friends from the early days of my scooter life, we were a diverse group but with a common link that gave us a reason to spend time together and build long-lasting memories.

Some of those people would find life taking them in different directions and away from scooters, but with a resurgence of the scooter scene at the start of the 21st century, it was not unusual to bump into these old friends at local scooter ride outs and events. Some had never stopped riding while others would get back onto a scooter again after a break, brought on by bringing up families or having moved on from the scene for a while and finding other things to do with their time and money.

Sadly, we sometimes find ourselves reminiscing about friends that were not able to grow older with us. Following Dwain's tragic accident at the end of 1987, Carl Cartwright (builder of the white Lambretta cutdown with extended forks) died after an accident on his scooter in the early 1990s and soon afterwards Andy Hawes (Legend Lives On, Little Lamb Bee and Death in the Afternoon), finding things too much of a struggle, took his own life. John Edge died from a toxic reaction to some ecstasy he took in a night club and Tom Rix of the Desert Rats SC died some years later from cancer. These events can't be changed, I am just glad that they were able to enjoy the thrill of riding a scooter along with being involved in the scooter scene at a very special time, and that I was able to know them for a while too.

Beer and drinking have been mentioned frequently throughout this book. I would like to reassure anyone concerned about the number of times this national pastime is mentioned that you don't have to drink copious amounts of alcohol to qualify as a scooter rider (if any at all), it is just something that scooterists enjoy and do very well, and rightly or wrongly, drinking and the public house are deep-seated in British culture. Many scooterists don't need an excuse for a quick pint at the end of a day's riding, but I can testify that taking that first sip of chilled beer after a long day in the saddle is a most delicious and refreshing moment.

The future is unwritten, nobody knows what is just around the corner, but sometimes we can affect it. Earlier this year (2023) a chance encounter with someone where I live resulted in me buying a Spanish Eibar Lambretta LD125, made sometime between 1956 and 1958. Despite having a fondness for these old machines, I never thought about owning one as the engines are vastly different to those in later Lambrettas and they are VERY slow, too slow I feel for modern traffic.

Minty the Imperial, who knows where this one will take me

However, after it was mentioned that it was in its original condition and might be for sale, then seeing some pictures of the scooter, I couldn't not buy it. She looked lovely and because of its well-worn but original 1950s green paint, it was immediately given the name "Minty" by Kerry, much to my consternation. I saw sense though and Minty soon became "Minty the Imperial." She was given a thorough clean to remove over 60 years' worth of grime and Spanish muck, but the paintwork and all its history has been preserved and along with an engine rebuild, including a GT top end kit, electronic ignition and a long-awaited Booster exhaust, it should be much more usable on modern roads. She is a very different character to Solid Air and riding her is a steady and sedate affair that makes me think of supposedly simpler times. She will be ridden around the flatlands of Cambridgeshire, maybe even beyond, and I am looking forward to putting many relaxed and enjoyable miles on her engine in the future, who knows where she will take me.

I have taken part in many different aspects of scootering over the years. These experiences have given me many happy memories that are all down to owning and riding scooters, the places they have taken me to and the people that I have met along the way. I still have loads of enthusiasm and ideas for things to do with my scooters and places to ride them to, and while my body doesn't groan too much at the abuse it is given, I will keep on riding and enjoying my scooters for as long as I can.

MANY THANKS TO...

Kerry for inspiring me to write this book and for her encouraging enthusiasm every time she read the latest update. Paul Weller and The Jam for starting it all off, even though I didn't realise it at the time. That film. My dad for being the guarantor and signing the necessary papers so that I could buy my first scooter. Nigel Sleightholm, for reading and helping to edit this book, for providing ideas and for sharing my enthusiasm, as well as being a bloody good bloke, who, along with Paul Thomson, invited me to go racing with them as part of Privateer Racing. Viv McCann, my best mate, for being there when needed and for helping to bring my scooter ideas to life.

Also, Andy Neville, for his ideas on how to start the book. Mark Brough, author of Time, Trouble and Money, for his advice and tips. Martin Bird at Bird Creative, for graphic design and layout. Martin "Sticky" Round, for his helpful advice. Rebecca Genery, for map and illustration inspiration. Tracy Round, for proofreading and Warren Smith, for picture editing help.

MANY THANKS ALSO TO...

Bill Smith for allowing me to reproduce images taken from the All Mod Cons LP. Design and Art Direction copyright Bill Smith. Album cover photography copyright Peter Gravelle.

BSEC logo reproduced with kind permission of Keith Terry.

Lambretta Club of Great Britain logos reproduced by kind permission of the LCGB.

Paddy Smith rally patch images reproduced with the kind permission of Annie Smith.

Scandi Raid logo designed and produced by Allan Tait and Colin Fitzgerald.

Many thanks also to the following people, for allowing their photos to be included in this book:

Billy Bye – page 136

Lee Hollick – page 187 and 198 (right)

Lorraine and Darren Holdsworth – page 125

Martin "Sticky" Round – page 191

Roy Hunter – pages 64 (right), 65, 82, 83 and 84

Tony O'Brien – page 200

Trevor Peat – pages 8, 38 and 72

All other photos supplied by the author.